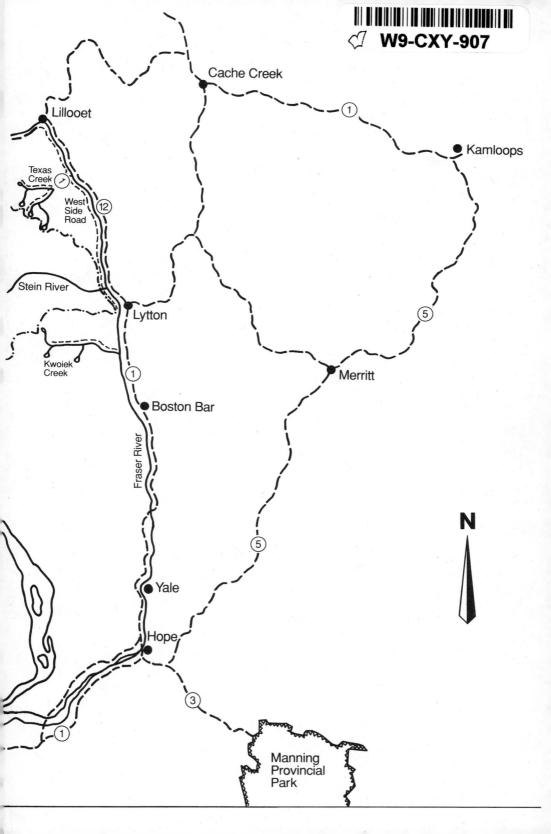

Cache Creek

Lillooet

Kamloops

Texas
Creek

West
Side
Road

12

Stein River

Lytton

Kwoiek
Creek

1

Boston Bar

Fraser River

5

Merritt

5

Yale

Hope

N

3

1

Manning
Provincial
Park

Stein Valley

Wilderness Guidebook

Gordon R. White

Stein Wilderness Alliance
Vancouver, B.C.

Canadian Cataloguing in Publication Data

White, Gordon R.
        Stein Valley Wilderness Guidebook

Includes bibliographical references.   ISBN 0-9694618-0-1

1. Stein River Valley (B.C.) - Description and travel -Guide-books. 2. Trails - British Columbia - Stein River Valley - Guide-books. 3. Outdoor recreation - British Columbia - Stein River Valley - Guide-books. 4. Natural history - British Columbia - Stein River Valley. I. Stein Wilderness Alliance (Vancouver, B.C.). II. Title.
FC3845.S84W55 1990   917.11'72   C90-091411-4
F1089.S84W55 1990

The Stein Wilderness Alliance's mailing address is:
2150 Maple St., Vancouver, B.C. V6J 3T3

Front cover photo: Martin Roland.
Rear cover photos, clockwise from top left: Leo deGroot, G.R. White, Pat Morrow, Gary Feighen.
Cover design and inside front cover map: Michael McInulty

This book was produced on an Ano computer using Microsoft Word and Aldus Pagemaker software. Printed and bound in Canada by Hignell Printing Ltd. Paper: 50% recycled (10% post-consumer), acid-free.

The following initials are used in the book for the photographic and illustrative credits.

J.A. - Jacques Andre	I.M. - Ian Mackenzie
N.B. - Neil Baker	M.M. - Mike McInulty
A.B. - Adelbert Beekmans	D.M. - David Montageau
L.d. - Leo deGroot	N.W.P.S. - Northwest Wildlife Preservation Society
A.D. - Adrian Dorst	
G.F. - Gary Feighen	R.B.C.M. - Royal B.C. Museum
F.S. - Five Seasons Adventure Tours	J.R. - June Ryder
T.H. - Terry Hale	S.W.A. - Stein Wilderness Alliance
R.H. - Rick Hewat	R.S. - Randy Stoltman
K.L. - Ken Lay	D.T. - David Thompson
L.V.E.C. - Lynn Valley Ecology Center	W.C.W.C. - Western Canada Wilderness Committee

This book is dedicated to all the people working to protect and enhance our planet's natural environment, and to Carman and Diane White.

"In saving wilderness, every victory could be temporary, every defeat is permanent."

Bristol Foster

Disclaimer:

This guidebook is intended to serve as a resource for recreational opportunities within and adjacent to the Stein River Valley; it should be used as a general guide only. Persons using this book do so with the understanding that the roads, trails, and routes described in this book are constantly changing. While every effort has been made to note the real and potential hazards found in the book's trails, routes, and roads, readers should be prepared for conditions other than those described. Neither the author nor the publisher is liable or responsible to any person or entity for any loss or damage caused or alleged to be caused directly or indirectly by the information contained in this guidebook.

TABLE OF CONTENTS

Acknowlegements

A special thanks to the B.C. Mountaineering Club, Mountain Equipment Co-op, Vancouver City Savings Credit Union, and the Alpine Club of Canada - Vancouver Section, whose financial support made this book possible.

Also providing assistance were the following major sponsors:

Additional support was provided by:

Alpine Club of Canada - Vancouver Island
Coghlan's
Michael Down
Ecosummer Expeditions
Ganapathi and Associates

New Roots Nutrition
Outbound
Gary Richter
Valley Outdoor Association

A special thanks goes to **Northwest Wildlife Preservation Society** for its timely contribution. **North Face** and **patagonia** provided assistance with equipment requirements.

Many people gave generously of their time, energy, and talent in producing this book. I apologize for any omissions from the following list. Assisting with correspondence & computers, providing encouragement and support, etc. were: Mark Bayntun, Alistair Blachford, Lindsay Brooks, Jackie Garnett, Jean Hamilton, Cecile Helton, Rick Hewat, Kara Jenne, Leo and Hilary McGrady, Deanna McLeod, Jennifer Nener, and Tony Ross. A special thanks goes to the staff at ANO Office Automation in Richmond. Neil Baker, Chris Bradley, and Leo deGroot provided valuable information for the skiing section of the book. My numerous trips to Lytton were made more enjoyable by Bud and Marion Wells' hospitality. Michael M'Gonigle, Wendy Wickwire, Roger Freeman, and David Thompson provided valuable support and advice.

Valuable editoral assistance was provided by Alistair Blachford, Blanca Chester, Lynn Deegan, Leo deGroot, Cecile Helten, Tim McGrady, Chris Parks, David Thompson, and Ronald White. All the contributors to the natural history information of this book are deserving of special recognition. Also assisting were Alistair Blachford, Dick Cannings, Ralph Cartar, Trevor Goward, and Don McPhail. Providing much needed feedback and assistance with the cultural history information were Chris Arnett, Nancy Turner, and Wendy Wickwire. Jennifer Nener's research and editorial work was especially helpful. This book's pictures and illustrations were provided by numerous individuals and organizations, in particular Neil Baker, B.C. Parks (North Vancouver), Leo deGroot, David Montageau, Royal B.C. Museum, and Western Canada Wilderness Committee. Jacques Andres' assistance with the picture selection was helpful. Many thanks to Tammy Knight for her always entertaining cartoons.

The production of this book was made financially possible by the generosity of the Stein Wilderness Alliance's supporters, and the above sponsors. Especially helpful was Tom Herbst's encouragement and assistance with fund-raising. Undoubtedly, this book would not be what it is if it were not for the help of the Institute for New Economics.

Finally, a few individuals warrant extra recognition. An extra special thanks to Mark McMillan and Pat Walker for their work on the maps, and John Bell, Janet Bruch, Kevin Harris, Jacqui Peachie, and Joan E. Vance for their book formatting work. Very special extra thanks go to Michael McInulty for his assistance with the layout and preparation of the final copy, cover design, and flora and fauna illustrations, and Chris Tunnoch for providing her wonderful vignette illustrations on such short notice.

PREFACE

Is the Stein important as "the last unlogged major watershed in Southwestern B.C," or as a source of fibre and jobs in an area short of timber? As a unique native heritage site with unequalled pictographs? As a largely untouched river valley with high biogeoclimatic and wildlife diversity? As a classic conflict between resource development and preservation? Answer: All of the above, and more.

For us, the Stein held no special initial interest. We were present when the decision was made to advocate a moratorium on development. But we needed to see it for ourselves, not from a helicopter as some parks and forest service civil servants did, but as an extended immersion experience. Crossing the entire watershed in 10 days from near Lillooet Lake to Lytton, we sat by a campfire one night in the Raven Flats and expressed our growing commitment to preserve the Stein's values from the usual fate: "There has to be a way - we must find it."

How that long and tortuous way was found by us and others is an unusual and largely unknown story, showing how difficult it is to judge what will work. In 1975 environmentalists had very little clout. But we believed that because of the large side-valleys that were impractical to log, the valley would still be valuable even if (as a whole) it could not be preserved. Though we lost the first battle (at the time of the switch from the Barrett to the Bennett government), we succeeded in getting the Minister to establish an advisory committee. While driving from Vancouver to meetings in Lytton we sometimes wondered whether it was worthwhile to work under a repugnant development decision. When a major procedural controversy developed, we were able to argue successfully for an 18 month moratorium on the final development decision; unexpectedly that period overlapped the Wilderness Advisory Committee process that led to the consequent decision to require an agreement with the Lytton Indian Band. The rest is history, and the Stein remains to this day unlogged (and hopefully politically unloggable).

Since then the ease of access to and within the valley has changed from what we described in our now out-of-print 1979 guidebook, *Exploring the Stein River Valley*. The improvement and paving of the Duffey Lake Road will soon bring countless people within easy distance of the Stein watershed boundary. The appearance of this guidebook is therefore timely. We hope you who will use it to explore the valley will come to share some of our love for the Stein.

Roger D. Freeman and David Thompson

INTRODUCTION

Embracing the transition zone between B.C.'s cool, wet Coastal rainforests and hot, dry Interior plateau is the Stein River Valley, a 1060 square kilometre watershed of ecological and cultural wealth. Strikingly apparent to even the first time visitor is the Stein's completeness and diversity.

Its completeness is evident in that it is an intact watershed ecosystem - a land area drained by one river and consisting of integrated ecosystems that link together to form a single unit. In the valley, nestled between peaks and ridges, are Ponderosa pine benchlands, remnant glaciers, roaring river canyons, sparkling alpine lakes, floodplain cottonwood forests, broad alpine meadows, and rich coastal Western Hemlock forests. This diverse landscape in turn supports an abundance of wildlife, including cougar, bear, wolf, weasel, eagle, and owl.

A strong case for preservation can be made on these attributes alone. Yet the Stein is more than just beautiful wilderness. It contains numerous cultural heritage sites of the Nlaka'pamux People who used the valley for thousands of years as a spritual retreat. The culturally modified trees, pictographs, and caves speak of another time when man was part of the whole web of nature, rather than removed from it like modern day man.

The forest industry and provincial government, however, have treated the Stein like every other valley in B.C. - a timber supply that must be accessed at all costs. We are only beginning to learn the secrets of the ancient forests and yet the remaining old-growth forests are being liquidated at an unprecedented and unsustainable rate. To protect the Stein as a wilderness reserve is not only to maintain a living classroom which nurtured the native people for thousands of years, but also to leave a remnant of the original landscape for future generations.

Less tangible, but of equal importance, is the need to provide space for other inhabitants of this planet. In other words, wildlife needs wilderness. One need look no further than the Stein's surrounding valleys to discover that the Stein watershed has become a refuge for, among others, cougar, grizzly, and wolverine - animals that require large tracts of undisturbed land. If we are to reverse the current rate of exterminating 20 species a day, protection of habitat like the Stein is essential.

The primary intent of this book is to assist people in visiting the Stein. Once you have experienced this valley - whether it be relaxing by the meandering river in the lush mid-valley, watching with wonder a grizzly wandering carelessly across the alpine meadows, or standing fascinated by the pictographs of the lower canyon - the case for protecting the Stein is obvious. You will also discover what has been known to the Nlaka'pamux for thousands of years: Both as individuals and as a society, we have so much to learn from the Stein. Many people, such as myself, who have repeatedly visited the valley, have come to eagerly await every return trip, for, as in life, there is so much to learn and enjoy.

Of course, it goes without saying that the Stein is also a place of rejuvenation, which in our increasingly complex world is needed more than ever. To leave the latest technological mysteries behind and experience the basic cycles of life is to regain a sense of place with the natural world and cleanse one's body, mind, and soul.

Unfortunately, as more and more people experience and learn from this valley, a more benign form of destruction threatens the Stein; backpackers not practising minimal impact camping may slowly destroy the wilderness character of the Stein. One of the underlying themes of this book is the importance of educated backcountry travel. Read the **Before You Go** section of this book, which discusses the fundamentals of responsible wilderness travel, and tread lightly when travelling through the Stein.

Many of the valley's more prominent residents have been highlighted to help convey the uniqueness and diversity of the Stein's flora and fauna. Hopefully in exploring the Stein with this book, the reader will learn more of not only this valley but of other valleys which are also threatened.

I hope that people learn from the Stein. The most immediate lesson to be gained is that both as individuals and as a global society we must change our attitudes and values. Out of this transformation will hopefully come many changes, one of the most important being the awareness and action needed to help protect not only the Stein but the many other endangered wilderness areas. One can only hope that this transformation will take place. For if we are not able to set aside unique areas of ecological and cultural wealth like the Stein, the future of planet Earth and its inhabitants is bleak.

Gordon R. White
July, 1991

HOW TO USE

THIS GUIDEBOOK

HOW TO USE THIS GUIDEBOOK

In order to protect areas of special ecological value and allow for individual exploration, some regions of the Stein have not been described in this book. With only a few exceptions, however, all the trails and routes described in *Exploring the Stein River Valley* have been included. Plus, several new routes in the Cottonwood Creek drainage have been added. Mountaineering routes and access are not described. See Bruce Fairley's *Climbing and Hiking in Southwestern B.C.* for information on the peaks within and adjacent to the Stein watershed. Those wanting a quick summary of the trips described in this book should consult the trip summary component of this section.

Given the Lytton and Mt. Currie Bands' concerns, information on only a few of the more accessible cultural heritage sites throughout the valley has been included. The observant hiker should be able to recognize and locate other sites.

Please keep in mind that this book is only a guide; it is by no means a substitute for common sense, sound judgement, and preparedness. Please inform me of any errors so that corrections can be made in subsequent editions. Constantly changing conditions due to fire, windfall, landslides, avalanches, erosion, etc. can quickly change the trail and routes described in this book - be prepared for the unexpected. Take the time to read this section so that you are familiar with the format and terms used in this book.

BOOK STRUCTURE

This book is divided into seven parts.

Part I - Road Access - provides information on the various access points and roads to the Stein Valley. This section is intended to be used with the inside front cover map. Be sure to read this section for precautions such as active logging and potential wash-outs.

Part II - Cultural History - is a brief account of the Stein Valley's human history.

Part III - Natural History - describes the ecology, geology, vegetation, birds, fish, and mammals of the valley.

Part IV - Before You Go - is a very important section and should be read carefully by novice and experienced hikers alike. The ethics, precautions, preparations, and equipment involved in wilderness travel are covered.

Part V - Recreational Information - provides information on backpacking, ski-touring, and kayaking.

Part VI - The Politics of Preservation - looks at the politics involved in protecting wilderness areas in B.C. such as the Stein.

Part VII - contains an index and selected bibliography.

TRAIL AND ROUTE LEGENDS

A legend at the beginning of each hiking trail or route description summarizes the essential information for that particular trip. These points are not necessarily repeated in the text of the description, so ensure that you read the summary carefully. Most hikes will encompass more than one trail and/or route description. Given the considerable variation in cautions, water availability, etc. among individual trails and routes, it is important to read the summaries of all the trails and/or routes you plan to travel. The terms used in the legends are as follows:

Attractions refer to any distinguishing characteristics including scenery, wildlife, good campsites, the best siesta sites, and other specific highlights.

Cautions list possible dangers or concerns that you should be aware of before setting out on the trip such as dangerous terrain, unpredictable weather conditions, water availability, wildlife habitat, and devious rodents. These cautions are not repeated in the main text of the trip description and should be carefully noted, particularly by less experienced hikers.

Access is the starting point for the trail or route. Refer to the enclosed fold-out map of the Stein and the inside front cover map of southwest B.C. to locate the various trails, routes, and access roads described in this book.

Season is usually the best time of year for the trip. The months are given in approximate ranges and can vary depending on the weather and snowpack in any given year. Remember, in the alpine, weather can change quickly at any time of the year. At lower elevations, especially in the eastern part of the valley, it may be possible to hike from February to November without encountering snow. Some parts of the Stein's alpine receive heavy snowfall, especially on the western half of the watershed; the melting of the winter snowpack will depend on the depth of snow and spring weather conditions. North and east-facing slopes are usually the last to be snow-free, so take this into account when planning your trip.

Rating refers to the approximate difficulty of the trail or route. These ratings are based on an adult in reasonable shape (exercises at least three times a week and is comfortable carrying a multi-day pack). The ratings give the ease of travel over the terrain, but they do not convey specific hazards and problems for that trail or route. Read the **Cautions** in the legend for this information. Remember that changing conditions can alter these estimates. The following is a general guide to the three ratings:

Easy - even terrain; minimal elevation change (less than 30 m gain per km); clearly marked trails; half-day or day trips. Suitable for novice hikers in average or lower than average physical condition.

Moderate - some rough terrain; moderate elevation change (30 m - 150 m gain per km); route-finding may be required; day trips or overnight backpacking. For intermediate or advanced hikers in average physical condition.

Difficult - Rough, sometimes exposed, terrain; substantial elevation gain and/or change (more than 150 m gain per km) may be required; may involve bush-whacking for part of trip; route finding with a compass is a possibility; often an overnight trip with a heavier pack (the Traverse would be classified as difficult since one must carry at least a 17 - 22 kg (35 - 50 lb.) pack for six to ten days, often over rough terrain). Best left to experienced hikers in good physical condition with some degree of masochistic inclination.

Distances are stated in metric with Imperial equivalents in parentheses. Trail and route distances were derived either by direct measurement using a trail wheel or from large scale (1:50,000) topographical maps.

Time is given in a range to provide a useful guide for hikers of varying abilities and conditioning. **Unless otherwise indicated, the time is ONE-WAY only.** Record your time along the trail and be prepared to alter your plans if you are taking longer than the high end of the range or if conditions are different than expected. Remember that large groups generally are slower than small ones, river or creek crossings may consume extra time for the inexperienced, and hikers not accustomed to hot weather should not expect to move at their normal speed in summer.

Elevation gain is noted for any appreciable gain in elevation along the trail or route. This number is the total vertical distance the trail or route climbs one-way and is derived from 1:50,000 topographic maps with 30 m (100 ft) contour intervals.

Accumulative elevation change is included where the accumulative vertical ascents and descents on the trail or route are enough to merit mention. This figure refers to the total vertical change over the trail or route, including downhill as well as uphill travel. For example, if a route gains 900 m (3000 ft) and then descends 450 m (1500 ft), the accumulative elevation change is 1350 m (4500 ft). This term has been included to give the reader a better understanding of the terrain one will encounter when travelling that particular trail or route. The majority of backpackers find large successive vertical gains and drops to be the most tiring, especially for those with arthritic joints; hence the need to include it.

Map refers to the number of the Energy, Mines and Resources Canada topographical map (1:50,000 series) covering the area of the trail or route. A distinction is drawn in this guide between trails and routes. Trails are cleared and marked while routes require topo map reading and, less frequently, compass assisted travel. **All route descriptions should be used with the 1:50,000 maps, and where applicable, the one page maps. The fold-out map included with this guide is intended to give an overview of the Stein Valley and its access points; it should not be considered a replacement for a topo map.**

In the lower mainland, topo maps can be reliably obtained from the Geological Survey of Canada (Suite 600, 100 West Pender Street, Vancouver V6B 1R8, (604) 666-1271), World Wide Books and Maps (736A Granville Street, Vancouver V6Z 1G3, (604) 687-3320), and Nixons Book Store (659 Columbia Street, New Westminster V3M 1L8, (604) 521-2810). In Victoria, try Earth Quest Books (1286 Broad Street, Victoria V8W 2A5,

(604) 361-4533). In places other than southwest B.C., try local bookstores or ordering from the above outlets.

Place names. Official and unofficial place names are differentiated in this book differently than in the fold-out map. In the book, those names which have been accepted by the Canadian Permanent Committee on Geographic Names are printed in regular typeface. Unofficial names are put in quotations in the table of contents and the trail and route headings. Unofficial place names identified within the text but not listed in the trail or route headings are also put in quotations. The fold-out map differentiates official and unofficial names by typestyle: Unofficial names are in calligraphy while official names are in type. Whenever possible, Indian names have been referenced in the text.

TRIPS SUMMARY

To assist you in choosing a trip, many of the more popular trails and routes described in this guide are organized below according to trip time. Use the fold-out map and the trail and route legends to determine the location of the trip and its access. You will want to account for travel time to and from the Stein, especially when using the less accessible roads.

1. Day trips

The Stein's lower canyon sees the vast majority of hikers visiting the Stein because of its easy access, accommodating terrain, and cultural richness. Other parts of the watershed offer day trips, notably the Blowdown Pass area, but they are not as easily accessed and have more demanding terrain. If you want a day or weekend of easy hiking, the lower canyon is your best bet, particularly for groups with children.

Less than half-day (round trip):

Lower Stein
Trips 1, 2, 4, and 8 (Trailhead to Devil's Staircase).

Siwhe Creek - Cattle Valley
Trip 24.

Blowdown Pass - Cottonwood Basin
Trips 31, 34, and 35.

Lizzie Lake to Lizzie Cabin
Trip 16.

Half-day to full day (round trip):

Lower Stein
Trips 5,6,7, and 8 (long day trip).

Siwhe Creek - Cattle Valley
Trip 23.

Blowdown Pass - Cottonwood Basin
Trips 32 and 36.

North Stein
Trips 42 and 43.

2. Weekend trips (2 - 3 days round trip):

Lower Stein
Trips 8, 9 - Trailhead to Ponderosa Creek. For faster hikers or long weekends,
Cottonwood Creek , trip 10, is possible.

Siwhe Creek - Cattle Valley
Trips 23, 24, 25, and 28 (to Earlobe Lake).

Blowdown Pass - Cottonwood Basin
Trips 31 - 39. One moderately difficult loop trip of 3 days encompasses trips
31, 33, 39, and part of 38 (see fold-out map).

North Stein
Trips 42 - 45.

3. Extended Backpacking (more than 3 days):

Longer trips inevitably pose a problem for hikers. A round- trip may involve travelling
over the same terrain twice but it does permit you to avoid transportation problems. One-
way trips, however, are logistically more complicated since you must arrange for
transportation at both ends - the price you pay to see new country during the entire trip. Be
sure to read the **Road Access** section of this book for information and ideas on how
to arrange for transportation at one or both ends of a one-way trip. A few phone calls to
local taxi operators in the towns closest to your entry and exit points may prove to be
very useful.

For those wanting to experience the Stein's unique diversity, two different one-way trips
are recommended. The eight to twelve day traverse of the watershed from its headwaters
to its confluence with the Fraser (or vice-versa) is the obvious choice for seeing the Stein's
alpine, subalpine, mid-valley forests, and lower canyon.

Stein Traverse

Overview

The complete traverse description has been split in two for the benefit of the majority of
hikers who enter the Stein from the east or west ends but do not actually hike the entire
traverse. The eastern half, Stein Trailhead to Stein Lake, is described from **east to west**.

Lizzie Lake to Stein Lake, the western half, is described from **west to east**. This means that those hiking the entire traverse will have to read part of the descriptions in reverse.

It is now possible to hike from the Trailhead near Lytton to Stein Lake along a cleared and well-marked trail. The alpine route from Lizzie Lake to Stein Lake requires route-finding, despite attempts to mark the way with cairns. Those seeking a more lengthy and demanding trip that allows one to experience the different climatic zones, landscape, vegetation, and wildlife within the valley will find the 75 km traverse to be the answer.

Requirements

The demands of hiking the full length of the valley should not be underestimated. Unpredictable weather, steep ascents and descents, and rough terrain are part of the hike, especially in the western half. You should be in good shape and properly equipped; if you find the West Coast Trail to be demanding, do not even think about this trip. Solid route-finding skills are an absolute necessity: the weather can change quickly, sometimes resulting in a whiteout, requiring travel by compass. Remember, once at Stein Lake, the halfway point, you are at least two days from any assistance.

Logistics

While it is possible to hike the traverse from the east or west, transportation is most easily arranged by driving to Lizzie Lake, leaving your car there, taking the bus home from Lytton, and then retrieving your vehicle from Lizzie Lake. To minimize pollution, leave your car at home and take the bus or train to Pemberton; B.C. Rail and Maverick Coach Lines serve this small farming community north of Whistler. At Pemberton, local taxi service is available (Alliance Taxi and Limousine, (604) 894-6565 for smaller groups and Tracker Trips, (604) 894-6161 for larger groups) to take you the 46 km from downtown Pemberton to the Lizzie Lake parking lot. At the east end, Greyhound Bus Lines serves Lytton three times a day (an eight km hike or drive from the Trailhead to town is necessary). Travelling west to east is also favoured for its drop in elevation from the alpine to the valley bottom. Conversely, starting at Lytton allows you to lighten your pack and strengthen your legs before tackling the much rougher western section.

Time and season

Plan on at least seven days; ten to twelve days is ideal. This allows you to experience rather than just visit the valley. The high snowfall on the western half of the Stein limits the traverse season from mid-July to late September.

The "Mini Traverse"

Hikers with less time, energy, experience, and pain tolerance but still intent on visiting the various ecological zones should consider what I call the "Mini Traverse." This three to six day trip takes you from Blowdown Pass to Cottonwood Creek and then out via the mid-valley and lower canyon to the Trailhead near Lytton (trips 38, 41, 10, 9, and 8). See the fold-out map for an overview.

Other trips

To fully experience what, in large part, makes the Stein different from most of B.C.'s parks (an unlogged valley bottom!), an eight day round trip from the Trailhead to Stein Lake and back is recommended. Variations on the "Mini Traverse" are possible, as there are numerous routes on the Stein's northern alpine boundaries. Once again, the fold-out map will give you a good overview.

PART I:

ROAD ACCESS

ROAD ACCESS

Access to the trails and routes described in this book is possible through the roads described below. Special care is necessary when travelling the logging roads that give access to the Stein. Road construction, washouts, and logging affect distances and access points. This is especially relevant for the Duffey Lake Road, which at the time of printing was being graded and paved. Allow for variations in road conditions.

Areas currently being logged or scheduled for further cutting have been indicated. When in doubt, you may want to check with the Ministry of Forests and the logging companies (see individual road description for specific numbers) before driving on certain roads. During the warmer months there may be restrictions on travel due to fire closures. Note: The distances given are accurate, but allow for 0.25 km error. **Also, the road descriptions are meant to be used with the inside front cover map, which shows the locations of the roads relative to the Stein.**

Of considerable concern to every weekend backcountry explorer is the prospect of encountering a logging truck on a tight bend of road. These trucks have limited maneuverability and often operate dawn to dusk seven days a week. Be sure to give them the right of way and exercise extreme caution when approaching blind curves, switchbacks, and narrow sections. Park your automobile well to the side of any road that is travelled by logging trucks. Gravel and dirt roads take a toll on your automobile so be prepared. Ensure you have sufficient gas - consumption is much higher on these roads since travel is often in low gear. A spare tire and jack are essential. Basic tools, a shovel, and jumper cables are recommended.

Lower Stein via Lytton

Situated on the Fraser River 260 km (160 mi) from Vancouver, 76 km (48 mi) from Cache Creek, and 164 km (102 mi) from Kamloops, the Town of Lytton gives you access to the Stein's Lower Canyon, Highway #12 between Lillooet and Lytton, and the West Side Road. Downtown Lytton is accessed via exits from the Trans-Canada Highway both north and south of town. If approaching the town from the south, look for the turnoff at the junction with an ESSO service station (you should see highway signs indicating this turnoff as the road to Highway #12). Similarly, from the north look for signs indicating access to Highway #12 and Lytton. Both these turnoffs bring you onto a road that runs through Lytton, becoming Main Street.

Your starting point once downtown is the "heart of Lytton," the junction of Main Street and 6th Avenue. At this junction you will find a sign indicating the route to Highway #12, the post office, the R.C.M.P. station, and the Lytton Hotel (and pub). Lytton also has several stores and hotels. Please support the local businesses. The only public transportation to and from Lytton is the bus, which stops two blocks south of 6th Avenue. Taxi service to the Trailhead is also available - enquire at the Lytton Hotel.

Downtown Lytton to Ferry

Starting from the junction of Main Street and 6th Avenue, proceed one block west towards the river to the junction of 6th Avenue and Fraser (follow the signs indicating Highway #12). Then proceed north descending to cross the railroad tracks and across the bridge over the Thompson River as you begin travelling Highway #12.

	km	mi
Junction of Main Street and 6th Avenue	0.0	0.0
Cross railroad tracks	0.2	0.1
Bridge over Thompson River	0.4	0.3
Botanie Valley road on right	0.9	0.6
Turn left onto Lytton Ferry access road, leaving Highway #12	1.1	0.7
Lytton Ferry	2.0	1.3

This reaction ferry - powered by the force of the river - accommodates two vehicles and is free. As of the time of printing the ferry's year-round operating schedule was: 6:30 a.m. to 10:15 p.m. with half-hour breaks at 10:30 a.m. and 6:30 p.m. The ferry serves vehicles on a first come basis with waits of more than 5 minutes being rare. Note: The ferry may not operate during high water in spring. Contact B.C. Highways, (604) 660-9770, for a status report when in doubt.

Lytton Ferry (T.H.)

Lytton Ferry to Stein Trailhead

	km	mi
Start on the west side of the Fraser	0.0	0.0
Road intersecting from left	0.6	0.4
Earlscourt Farm on left	1.4	0.9
Sharp bend in road	4.0	2.5
Turnoff to Stein Trailhead	4.8	3.0

Stein Trailhead

At the time of writing, access to the main Stein trail is possible by driving the 1.0 km road from the West Side Road to the parking lot at the Trailhead. This access crosses reserve property and should be respected as private property. **Permission is not required to cross at present, but this may change in the future.** At the Trailhead, which is not on reserve property, you will find ample parking. Ensure that your vehicle is locked and all valuables are removed.

The Trailhead access road is indistinguishable from the numerous other roads intersecting the West Side Road. Be sure to follow the above distances from the ferry.

	km	mi
Trailhead road leaves West Side Road	0.0	0.0
Pass remains of home and descend down side of hill.	0.2	0.1
Road on left; pass under hydro lines	0.5	0.3
Trailhead parking lot	0.9	0.6

West Side Road

A rough, winding gravel road that runs along the west side of the Fraser River from south of Boston Bar north to Lillooet, the West Side Road may be used if you desire an alternate route to Lillooet or if the ferry is not working (you must drive north to Lillooet via Highway #12 and then return south on the West Side Road). The 68 km (42 mi) of Highway #12 to Lillooet, on the east side of the Fraser, is faster, more scenic, and safer, however. Also, the West Side Road is muddy until mid to late June. Do not even think about travelling on the section south of the Lytton Ferry towards Boston Bar unless you have a four-wheel drive vehicle.

	km	mi
Lytton Ferry, west side of Fraser	0.0	0.0
Road intersecting from left	0.6	0.4
Earlscourt Farm on left	1.4	0.9
Sharp bend in road	4.0	2.5
Turnoff to Stein Trailhead	4.8	3.0
Stein Bridge	5.6	3.5

	km	mi
Junction in road, stay left	6.7	4.2
Bridge over creek	18.0	11.3
Sharp switchback in road. Access Siwhe Creek trail here.	24.1	15.0
Bridge over Siwhe Creek	25.4	16.0
McPhee Creek	40.0	25.0
Texas Creek Road on left	46.8	29.3
Junction of Duffey Lake road and West Side Road (marked as Texas Creek Road)	64.3	40.2
Lillooet townsite approximately 1.5 km north		

Texas Creek Road

Located 19.8 km (12.5 mi) south of Lillooet, the Texas Creek logging road provides access to the Siwhe Creek - Cattle Valley and "Brimful Lake" alpine areas. The road is in good shape with only a few rocky sections. Travel with caution - logging trucks may be on the road due to active logging in the Skimath Creek branch of Texas Creek (phone the Lillooet Forest District, (604) 256-7531, for current road status).

The start of the Texas Creek road is clearly marked with a Ministry of Forests sign, rest area, and bridge.

	km	mi
Leave West Side Road and follow the road into the steep-sided lower canyon of Texas Creek	0.0	0.0
Cross Texas Creek	0.1	0.1
Cross Texas Creek again	2.2	1.4
Molybdenite Creek Road on right	7.8	4.9
Cross Molybdenite Creek	8.7	5.5
Skimath Creek branch road on left; stay right.	12.7	8.0
Junction. Take left road to East Fork (right hand road is West Fork).	17.4	11.0
Junction. Follow road to right for 0.2 - 0.3 km if going to Brimful Lake area.	22.3	14.0

Left hand road extends 0.3 km, ending in wide turnaround. Access to hikes in the Siwhe Creek-Stein Divide are gained here.

Duffey Lake Road

Originally a forest access road, this 95 km road connects Pemberton and Lillooet and must be travelled when using the Blowdown and Van Horlick access points. Also, if travelling from areas east and north of the Stein, you may want to use this shortcut to gain entrance to the Lizzie Creek access on the west side of the Stein. Note: In the fall of 1989 paving of the Duffey Lake Road began. The entire road is to be graded and paved by the end of 1991. Changes in distances and access points will undoubtedly result. Despite fairly high avalanche dangers, the Highways Ministry is now maintaining this road year round. Carry chains, jumper cables, and a shovel when travelling the Duffey Lake Road from November to April, however.

Several B.C. Forest Service campsites are located on the Duffey Lake Road. These sites offer little more than cleared campsites and are often crowded on summer weekends. No other services are found on the Duffey Lake Road. Be sure to fill up before leaving Pemberton/Mt. Currie or Lillooet.

	km	mi
Junction at terminus of Highway #99	0.0	0.0
(1.0 km west is Pemberton townsite)		
Mount Currie; junction with road north to	6.7	4.2
D'arcy		
Junction of Duffey Lake Road and road	16.7	6.8
down the east side of Lillooet Lake to		
Lizzie Creek		
Joffre Alpine Recreation Site	29.2	18.3
Casper Creek Logging Road on south	41.3	25.8
Van Horlick Road on south (2 entrances)	42.1	26.3
Duffey Lake Recreation Site	48.2	30.1
Junction with Blowdown Logging Road	51.6	32.3
on right		
Roger Creek Recreation Site	64.1	40.0
Bridge across Cayoosh Creek	65.0	40.6
Cottonwood Recreation Site	73.4	45.9
Cinnamon Recreation Site	76.7	48.0
Junction with road to Seton Lake	91.6	57.3
Junction with West Side Road	95.1	59.4
(marked as Texas Creek Road)		

Lillooet townsite is approximately 1.5 km further north.

Located on the eastern end of the Duffey Lake Road, near the Fraser River, the town of Lillooet can provide most essential goods and services, and is served by B.C. Rail. Pemberton and Mt. Currie, at the western end, offer fewer services; Whistler, 30 minutes to the south on Highway #99, offers a greater variety of goods and services. Pemberton is served by both B.C. Rail and Maverick Coach Lines.

Blowdown Logging Road to Blowdown Pass

The Blowdown Logging Road provides access to the most accommodating alpine area in the Stein watershed. Normally fine for two-wheel drive vehicles, this well-travelled access is susceptible to spring runoff and may soon be impassable from as close as two km from the Duffey Lake Road. Contact the Lillooet Forestry office at (604) 256-7531 for road condition information.

A retractable road barrier lies approximately 60 m west of the intersection of the Duffey Lake and Blowdown roads. Look for a "No-Thru Road" sign at the beginning of the road. A series of switchbacks quickly brings you within sight of the Blowdown Creek trench. The road continues at a lesser grade on the east side of the creek for the remainder of the distance. This main road is clearly discernable from the numerous haul lines and branch roads that intersect it.

	km	mi
Intersection of Duffey Lake and Blowdown Roads	0.0	0.0
Road on left	0.3	0.2
Road on right	2.5	1.5
Road on right	5.3	3.3
Branch road to west side of Blowdown Creek	8.4	5.2
Junction and large level parking area Take left branch and begin to climb.	9.7	6.0
First of two switchbacks and beginning of private mining road. Park here.	11.2	6.9

Blowdown Pass is now 3.7 km (2.6 mi) further and 525 m (1750 ft.) higher. Several streams cross the road, providing a welcome respite on hot days. The route is easily followed as you move along the road towards the pass. At 2045 m (6800 ft.) and 1 hour - 1 hour 30 minutes from the parking area, the access to Blowdown Lake is met. Descend 45 m (150 ft.) through the meadows to the lake, which is only 0.3 km (0.2 mi) from the road. Numerous camping spots are found at this popular spot. The pass is now only 0.7 km (0.4 mi) distant, offering access to many fine alpine rambles and great views.

Van Horlick Logging Road

This road, which is also accessed from the Duffey Lake Road, gives access to the North Stein via Van Horlick Pass. Two-wheel drive vehicles should not have any problems with this road except in the wetter months of spring and the steep ascent starting at the east fork turnoff at 8.9 km (5.5 mi) Note: The regrading, widening, and paving of the Duffey Lake Road may alter the entrance to the Van Horlick Road - be sure to locate the proper access.

	km	mi
Junction with Duffey Lake Road	0.0	0.0
Junction; keep left	2.1	1.3
Junction; keep right	3.1	1.9
Cross bridge over creek	6.1	3.9
Junction; keep right	6.3	3.9
Junction; keep left	7.6	4.9
Major fork; go left, uphill	8.9	5.5
Branch road on right	10.9	6.8
Junction; logging road on right	12.2	7.6
End of road	15.3	9.5

Lizzie Creek to Lizzie Lake

A popular recreation area that has become busier with the increased interest in the Stein, the Lizzie Lake area provides access to the Stein's westernmost alpine and, of course, the Stein Traverse route. This is a rough road that will punish any vehicle - be sure to take an extra tire, jack, oil, belts, etc. The following begins at the intersection of the Duffey Lake and Lillooet Lake roads and proceeds south along the east side of Lillooet Lake.

	km	mi
Duffey Lake - Lillooet Lake roads junction	0.0	0.0
Cross bridge	0.3	0.2
Strawberry Point Forest Service Rec. Site	6.9	4.3
Road on left	9.6	6.0
Twin One Creek crossing	10.6	6.6
Twin One Creek Resort	11.6	7.3
Lizzie Bay Recreation Site	16.0	10.0
Bridge over Creek	16.5	10.3
Lizzie Creek Road on left; turn here	16.7	10.5
Junction; stay right	17.7	11.1
Road begins to steepen	24.7	15.8
Road becomes impassable for most two-wheel drive vehicles.	25.2	16.1

Some two-wheel drive vehicles can make it the extra 3.4 km (2.2 mi) to the lake where you will find a parking lot and rough campsites.

Public Transportation

One answer to our growing environmental crisis is reduced use of one's automobile, a major polluter and consumer of non-renewable resources. Viable alternatives for accessing the Stein are train and bus. Lytton is served by Greyhound Bus Lines ((604) 662-3222) while Lillooet is accessed by B.C. Rail ((604) 984-5264). Both B.C. Rail and Maverick Coach Lines ((604) 255-1171) serve Pemberton. Lytton is the only town that brings you within walking distance of the Stein, however. Taxi service is available in both Pemberton (see Traverse overview in **How To Use This Guidebook**) and Lillooet. Provided you can barter a reasonable price and divide the fare between several people, this is an alternative.

PART II:

CULTURAL

HISTORY

CULTURAL HISTORY

Native History

In the Beginning

One of the more recognizable and accessible pictographs found on the Stein's trails. (L.d.)

Modern anthropological explanations of the origins of North America's native peoples contrast sharply with the natives' own beliefs and mythology. The most accepted scientific explanation remains the migration of early ancestors from Asia to North America via a Bering Sea land bridge before the end of the last ice age, 10,000 years ago. Native people offer a different history which is consistent with their perception of life as an endless series of cycles. Since the Nlaka'pamux and other native people kept oral but not written records of their history, several explanations are given for the origin of the earth and its inhabitants. A great being figures prominently in these stories.

In one account, Old One created the earth from the soil of the upper world in which he lived. In other accounts, Old One, also referred to as Chief, Great Chief, or Big Mystery, created the earth from a woman. As recorded by James Teit, the ethnographer who lived with the Thompson People in the late 19th and early 20th centuries, the woman and her husband, the Sun, had an argument. As a result, the husband moved away from the woman to live with his relatives, the Moon and the Stars. Old One punished the husband and his relatives by transforming them into the heavenly bodies we know today and created the Earth from the woman.

Archeologists have reconstructed a rough sketch of the Nlaka'pamux pre-history. The earliest evidence of human habitation in south central B.C. indicates the presence of man approximately 9000 years ago. Close to the Stein, sites have been dated as far back as 6500 years. Establishing winter homes on the shores of the Fraser near its confluence with the Stein was a logical step for the Nlaka'pamux. A dependable salmon stream and accessible hunting and gathering areas in the nearby Stein and Botanie Valleys provided a dependable food supply. Besides offering food sources and an agreeable climate, the area surrounding the Stein was important in their mythology. The Nlaka'pamux attached considerable importance to the confluence of the Fraser and Thompson rivers just south of the Stein. This junction, called Lkamtci'n (today spelled Kumsheen), meaning "the forks" or "confluence," was central to native mythology as it was known as the center of the world.

Growth and Bonding

In the Nlaka'pamux world the individual was intrinsically linked to the larger group, the natural environment, and the spiritual world. These nurturing forces provided for the spiritual enrichment and development of the physical and psychological being of an individual. Conversely, western society's focus on individualism tends to isolate the individual from the community and the natural world.

Central to the individual's growth was a life-long process of traditional rituals. Children bathed in cold creeks or streams to develop discipline and a strong cardio-vascular system. During puberty, considered the most formative time for a Nlaka'pamux boy or girl, physical skills and spiritual values were refined. The individual became a fully-functioning member of his or her tribe's ancestral and spiritual worlds only at the end of puberty. Not only did the individual grow through these processes, but more importantly he or she acquired a strong sense and awareness of cultural identity.

A key element in this maturing and learning process was the development of a strong understanding of, and bond with, nature. This was achieved through isolation in remote parts of the mountains for periods of four months to a year or longer.

One important aspect of a youth's development was the quest for a guardian spirit. This search would begin when the youth travelled to a prominent peak or ledge above the river at dusk. After lighting a fire, and then singing and dancing until dawn, he or she eventually collapsed from physical exhaustion. In the dreams which followed, the spirits, which would give the youth life-long strength and protection, were revealed. The guardian spirit, a bird, animal, or other natural being, entered the youth's dream and spoke and sang. This song was of considerable importance at later times in the boy's or girl's life as it was used to summon his or her nature partner. By allying oneself with a "shna-am," one could then enter into a powerful, altered state known as "hah-hah," attaining special attributes such as great endurance and strength, immunity to danger, and the ability to change into other forms. Having gained special power through the spirit, the youth had completed his or her puberty experience and rituals.

Kinnikinnick
(*Arctostaphylos uva-ursi*)
The most common trailing evergreen in the Stein. Its bright red berries, which are in season from August to late winter, were used by native people for pemmican, and are a favorite of grouse and bear. The flowers are small, bell-shaped, and pink. Kinnikinnick means smoking mixture in Algonquin.
(B.C. Parks)

Today, the most visible evidence of these rituals in the Stein are the pictograph panels distributed throughout the lower valley. These paintings, drawn in a red paint made from a mixture of powdered rock and water, are found primarily in places known as power spots, where spirits resided. The caves, peaks (Mt. Roach, or "k'ek'azik," was one place of highly regarded power), high ledges, waterfalls, and lakes of the Stein were favoured for their special ambience, and also because they were secluded from the area of Kumsheen. Interpretation of these drawings is difficult since they were normally painted by a lone individual and reflected an individual's dreams or experiences not necessarily known to others.

Cycle of the Seasons

While a good portion of their time was spent hunting and gathering, tribal societies also

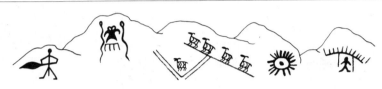

Pictographs of the Stein

The mythological and spiritual importance of the Stein River Valley is evident in the valley's concentration of native rock paintings. Indeed, over the years, archeologists and Lytton Band members have rediscovered no less than 13 rock painting sites along a 32 km (20 mi.) stretch of the river. They range in size from a single painting on a rock boulder to one of the largest rock paintings in Canada with almost 200 paintings rendered in red along the base of a cliff close to the river's edge.

Ethnographer James Teit was intrigued by the rock paintings and made numerous inquiries into their origin and function. Teit was told that the paintings:

"...were largely in the nature of records of the most important of the novice's experiences whilst training, such as things obtained or partially obtained as guardian spirits, things wished for or desired to be obtained, things actually seen during training or during vigils which were considered good omens [and/or] actual experiences or adventures of the novice, especially those in connection with animals."

"By making paintings of these things on

rocks the novices believed they would make such powers as they had attained or obtained stronger or more permanent and what they desired to attain (for instance, to be a shaman, warrior, proficient hunter, etc.) or to obtain (as for instance a certain guardian spirit, or certain powers or benefits) more easily and quickly obtainable."

Charles Hill-Tout, another early student of Nlaka'pamux culture, visited the Stein in the 1890s and was shown "certain spots and localities where celebrated shamans underwent their fasts and training to gain their powers." He was told that the paintings at these sites had been "made in the past by native shamans."

The paintings of owl, two-headed snake, grizzly bear, mountain top, and mystery lake that we see today on the banks of the Stein River are just some of the powerful guardian spirits witnessed in the dreams and visions of those shamans of long ago.

Not all rock paintings were made in the context of the guardian spirit quest. Some, according to information recorded by Teit:

"were made by both novices and adults of any age for what seems to have been chiefly

spent time enjoying recreational and artistic activities. Nlaka'pamux soapstone sculptures and ornate basketry and clothing designs suggest an artistically rich society. Storytelling, games, and gymnastics were regular activities.

To the Upper Nlaka'pamux, the year was divided into five seasons. The counting of the moons began when the marmots of the high country entered their dens, usually in November. During the first three moons (December - February) hunting and fishing became sporadic as the people moved into their winter pit houses at the mouth of the Stein and consumed preserved foods prepared the previous spring, summer, and fall.

protective purposes such as after a very striking dream or an event believed to portend evil, for the purpose of warding off the disaster or evil happenings."

These paintings, often representing guardian spirits, were painted on rock surfaces overlooking the route or trail "by which enemies or evil might approach. These pictographs by reason of their connection with the guardian spirits of the people who made them were believed to help in the protection of the latter." Other rock paintings were said to represent historical events and it is believed that some of the paintings in the Stein Valley are associated with incidents in the conflict between the Lil'wat (Mount Currie) and Nlaka'pamux (Lytton) peoples. And, as James Teit noted, still other paintings were believed to have been made not by humans but "are pictures made and shown by the mysteries, or powers, or spirits of the places where they are to be seen."

Teit's Nlaka'pamux informants told him that rock paintings had been made "from time immemorial." When he conducted his research at the turn of the century there were a number of elderly natives still living who *had made the pictographs. Teit concluded that the practice of rock painting began to decline around 1860 because of the increasing influence of non-native culture. He estimated that the majority of rock paintings "now to be seen" were created between 1800 and 1860. "But in some places," he added, "where the rock or their situations are favourable to the preservation of the paint, [the pictographs] no doubt are very much older."*

The rock paintings of the Stein, preserved in the wilderness environment which inspired their creation, are important to the preservation of native history and culture. They also serve as reminders to us all of our shared primordial past when humanity lived in close proximity to nature, dependent upon it for sustenance and spiritual well-being.

Chris Arnett

From this site, the people of Kumsheen had easy access to hunting and fishing in the Stein, sometimes venturing as far as Nesbitt Creek in search of deer and goat, rainbow trout, Dolly Varden char, and Rocky Mountain whitefish. In addition to accessible food sources, this winter site was close to water, fuel, and construction materials.

As the first edible shoots and spring salmon began to appear in March, the people moved out of the pit houses and recommenced hunting and gathering. If the salmon failed to come upriver, game was scarce, and winter food stores were depleted, famine became a possibility and the importance of root harvesting increased greatly. Avalanche lily, cow parsnip, Indian carrot, and thistle provided staple foods until the more readily obtainable summer food sources became available.

By the beginning of May, people began to gather food once again. Roots, corms, bulbs, and tubers were harvested primarily by the women, while the men hunted game and fished. The

The Role of Plants

The importance of plant foods in the traditional diet of the Thompson people is attested to by the fact that no less than 120 species of plants were utilized in some way as sources of foods, flavourings or beverages... The total of these various types is higher than 120, because many species yielded more than one type of food. Balsamroot, for example, provided edible roots, shoots and seeds. Thimbleberry, blackcap and salmonberry were used for *their edible shoots as well as for their fruits. In addition to these various species, at least 7 species were used for smoking, and at least 10 were specifically used in the preparation of foods, for lining and covering food containers or to surround food in cooking pits.*

Turner, Nancy, et al, *Thompson Ethnobotany*, Royal British Columbia Museum, 1990, p.19.

berry season would usually begin around the eighth month. The early berries such as wild strawberries, squaw currants, and some varieties of Saskatoon berries were followed by red huckleberries, soapberries, blueberries, wild gooseberries, and wild blackberries. The inner bark of Ponderosa and lodgepole pine, balsamroot seeds, hazelnuts, and Douglas fir sugar were harvested in the Stein's lower canyon and mid-valley.

In early fall, August and September, the Nlaka'pamux moved to harvest the salmon runs. Even today, many of the same catching, preparing, and drying techniques and equipment are used. In addition to salmon, a main winter staple, the Nlaka'pamux also harvested, dried and stored many plants. According to ethnobotanist Nancy Turner, each family may have picked more than 150 litres of berries and over 50 litres of roots. Despite this rate of harvest, the Nlaka'pamux were able to maintain bountiful plant populations. The continual cultivation of the soil that accompanied root harvesting, selective harvesting of larger roots, and periodic burning, enhanced the productivity of the land. Late blooming berries, autumn choke cherries, mountain-ash fruits, blue elderberries, black tree lichen, seeds of the whitebark pine, and many mushrooms were also harvested at this time. Oyster and pine mushrooms were two favorites found throughout the lower valley, while cedar bark and root were harvested in the fall.

Cow parsnip
(*Heracleum lanatum*)
The leafstalks and bud-stocks of this plant were an important spring time food source for native people. (R.B.C.M.)

Hunting, primarily of deer and goat, took many of the people to higher elevations in October and November. Grouse, hare or rabbit, squirrel, marmot, black and grizzly bear, beaver, duck, goose, and less frequently, lynx or coyote were also hunted. Between this hunting and the harvesting of alpine roots, such as avalanche lily and spring beauty, much of the group spent the summer and fall at higher elevations, returning only for short stays before settling in for the winter.

As the snow began to fall, the final kills were dried or smoked and transported back to the winter village. Once again, they returned to the main group and to their winter homes. The Nlaka'pamux aptly referred to this time as "going in time" (N'ulxtin). With the cold and snow making travel more difficult, this was the time for making clothing, baskets, and tools, playing games, and telling stories.

Ethnographic accounts suggest that this cycle of five seasons served the Nlaka'pamux well for thousands of years. Early explorers' journals like Simon Fraser's confirm that the Thompson People were healthy, rarely subject to disease, and lived long lives. The bond between the indigenous people and the land which had sustained them for so long was to be broken, however, as European settlers moved into the interior.

Western red cedar
(Thuja plicata)
Many of the cedar groves in the lower Stein contain culturally modified trees (C.M.T.s). These trees were used by Indians for shelter, clothing, and utensils, especially note-worthy of which were their water-tight baskets. (L.d.)

Contact

Contact with white people in 1808 changed life for the Nlaka'pamux forever. In less than 70 years the landscape was transformed from its natural state into a major transportation corridor. The traditional hunting and gathering areas which had sustained the native people were disrupted by the influx of white settlers who pre-empted large tracts of land for agriculture.

In 1812 a fur-trading post was established in Kamloops by the North West Company of Montreal. For the first time, Indians no longer acquired resources solely for their own use. Rather, the market forces of consumers far removed from the impact of over-trapping presented an endless demand for furs, which the natives exchanged for consumer goods such as blankets, guns, and jewelry. This fur trade was short-lived, however, because by the mid 1800s the once-plentiful fur-bearing animal populations were greatly depleted.

Another resource extraction boom of unprecedented magnitude began in 1858. Over 25,000 American prospectors descended upon Kumsheen and the surrounding area in search of gold. While the native people had managed to cope with the new people until then, they had no way of preparing for the onslaught of the miners. With no law enforcement agency in place, the impact of the miners was devastating. Families were disrupted as many native women and girls were abducted from their homes. Poor transportation systems made delivery of food supplies from the lower mainland difficult. The lack of food led to the plundering of native winter villages and food caches. Fights between Indians and whites inevitably ensued.

Settlement and Development

In its efforts to settle the interior, the colonial government gave priority to the construction of feasible transportation routes. The Harrison Trail, a route to Lillooet via the Fraser River to Port Douglas at the north end of Harrison Lake, and then to Anderson Lake and Lillooet, was established in the late 1850s. The Cariboo Wagon Road replaced the Harrison Trail upon its completion in 1864. Steamers began to ply the lower Fraser in the late 1850s.

Native people contributed to the building of these roads. But the breakup of families, neglect of their traditional hunting and gathering activities, and loss of food stores, resulted in upheaval and starvation for many. Adjusting to the changes proved difficult. Their plight was further compounded by a smallpox epidemic in 1862.

In 1860 Constable John Hill undertook the first official survey of the Stein. In search of a new mule trail, Hill travelled from Lytton to the Stein's western divide before turning back, concluding that the trail was unsuitable for mule travel. As the gold rush moved northward, settlement of the land became a priority for the colonial government. By the late 1870s small reserves were being surveyed for native people while white settlers obtained much larger tracts of the best land for farming. From this land allocation emerged a vibrant agriculture-based economy that was well established by the early 1870s. Native people became an integral part of the farms, taking work as farm labourers on local white farms to supplement their own small, subsistence farms. Unlike the previous short-term resource extraction booms, this renewable and community-based economy showed considerable promise. The diversity of crops included beets, barley, potatoes, hay, and cattle and dairy farming. This new agrarian way permitted some self-sufficiency within the community.

In 1882 the construction of the Canadian Pacific Railway began. While the railway was to bring increased prosperity to B.C., it provided few benefits to the Lytton area other than the short construction boom in 1884. The greater access to goods from distant markets that the railway provided was of greater concern to small interior communities such as Lytton. No longer did communities or regions need to be self-sufficient. Instead, specialization and large-scale production became essential in an increasingly international market. For smaller towns such as Lytton, achieving the scale of production necessary to compete was not always possible.

The most renowned farm of the Lytton area was Earlscourt Farm, a multi-crop farm from the 1850s through to the late 1910s. Under the direction of owner Thomas Earl, the B.C. interior's first fruit inspector, Earlscourt produced world class apples which were shipped as far away as London, England. In 1905, production reached a peak of 25 railcars of apples for export.

Post World War One

This changed after World War I as the labour intensive crops of grapes, apples, and beans could no longer compete with the large-scale farms of California and Washington. Less labour intensive alfalfa crops and livestock became the primary commodities, resulting in lower employment. This hurt the local native people who depended on the farms for work. In 1920 Earlscourt was sold to Colonel Spencer, who made Earlscourt famous for its purebred Herefords and prize bulls. The farm remained a strong economic force in the Lytton area until Spencer's death in 1960.

The construction of the Canadian National Railway from 1911 to 1914 had similar affects as the CPR 30 years earlier. For a short period, industry thrived and the population swelled. Upon completion, however, the workers moved on and supporting industries such as saw mills shut down. Agriculture again became the mainstay. Mining was a key player in the local economy throughout the late 1800s and early 1900s. From 1892 to 1911 gold was dredged on the Van Winkle Bar area on the Fraser by the Van Winkle Bar Hydraulic Company of Vancouver and the Fraser River Gold Dredging Company.

Tourists began to travel along the Cariboo Road to Barkerville with the completion of the Alexandra Bridge in 1927. Being a necessary mid-way stopover, Lytton benefitted. The upgrading of the Fraser Canyon Highway in 1964 greatly reduced Lytton's tourism industry, however. Commercial trapping returned to the Stein in the 1920s and 1930s, providing a livelihood for many native people until the crash of the fur market in 1938.

Post World War Two

With the decline of tourism and agriculture, and mining and trapping exhausted, the economy of the Lytton area suffered. Forestry was at the forefront of the post-war industrial expansion. By the early 1960s, mills were operating throughout the area as roads were pushed into virtually every valley. The Lytton mill was a welcome reprieve for what was now an economically depressed area. For the native people the local mill was an economic blessing as it provided badly needed jobs. Unfortunately, the timber companies opted for mass production in order to take advantage of the accessible forests in the surrounding area.

By the late 1960s, the Stein River Valley was also assessed for logging. By the early 1980s it was apparent that the companies were overcutting. As valley after valley was roaded and logged, the Stein stood untouched because of the natural barriers its lower canyon presented to road building (see **To Protect the Stein,** p. 180 for the political history of the Stein preservation campaign).

In addition to forestry, transportation became another economic force in the Fraser Canyon. The two railways and the Trans-Canada Highway made this area a major transportation corridor. Agriculture, while not as strong as before, was still a key component of the Lytton area's economy. The recent increase in Lytton's tourism may be an indication of Lytton's future given the area's accessible rivers and mountains.

Lytton Today

Despite limited land holdings and the cultural strife they have endured, the native people of Kumsheen retain many of their traditional ways. They continue to fish for salmon, gather mushrooms, pick berries, gather wild vegetables and traditional medicines, and hunt. The Lytton Band's efforts to protect the Stein and pursue its land claims has brought them into a new age. Recent political developments have seen both federal and provincial governments begin to slowly recognize the need to settle the question of aboriginal title and outstanding native land claims. Through its work on the Stein issue, the Lytton Indian Band has come to the forefront of the campaign to address these issues.

PART III:

NATURAL

HISTORY

ECOLOGY

Clinton Webb

Ecology, by definition, refers to the branch of science that studies the inter-relationships between living things and their physical environment. To many people, the word ecology also symbolizes the wisdom, beauty, and mystery underlying the workings of undisturbed nature. From the blossoming flowers in a sunny alpine meadow to the infinitely complex nutrient cycling system of an old growth forest, natural ecosystems embody a perfection and balance far beyond the design of human minds.

Ecology Basics

The patterns and structures of the Stein ecosystem, as with ecosystems everywhere else on the planet, grow out of the relationships between the plants and animals to their physical environment, specifically water, earth, and air:

water - precipitation (rainfall and snow)
- downslope surface water movement
- seepage through soil
- rivers, creeks, and lakes

earth - geological parent materials
- terrain
- soil types

air   - temperature
- wind

Of these, water is the major underlying force in both connecting the different parts of the ecosystems together as well as shaping the land. The sun's energy drives the endless water cycle in which the Stein watershed receives and releases moisture. In a sense, the Stein is a temporary holding area between falling precipitation and the Fraser River, which then transports the water back to the ocean. The rivers and streams transporting water through the watershed have carved V-shaped valleys out of millions of years old bedrock. Today, the flow of water continues to erode and transport soil particles and gravel from mountain tops to valley bottoms.

Seasonal freezing and thawing processes combine with other chemical interactions involving water in what is perhaps the most fundamental ecological process of all: The weathering of the bedrock to form soil particles and the release of dissolved nutrients into the soil. These nutrients are in turn absorbed by the roots of plants whose growth, death, and decay provide the basis of all the food chains and nutrient cycles of an ecosystem.

While the process of physical and chemical weathering of bedrock is known to be very slow, the actual weathering rates of different bedrock types under different conditions is largely unknown. It has been determined, however, that an inch of topsoil can take over a thousand years to form, and a fully developed forest soil, many thousands of years.

In addition to helping shape the land and form the soil, moisture received by the Stein watershed interacts chemically and physically with everything it comes in contact with. Falling precipitation exchanges nutrients and material with alpine rock and scrub, tree leaves and stems, shrubs, herbs, and, finally but most importantly, decomposing organic matter and soil of the forest floor. Watercourses of all sizes collect this surface water flow and underground water seepage, and in so doing respond to varying amounts of rainfall and snowmelt with fluctuating levels of flooding, erosion, and siltation.

At every point of its path through a watershed, the amount, nutrient composition, and purity of the water is the end product of the processes taking place all the way upstream to the mountain tops. In essence, water is the thread which connects a watershed, both functionally and symbolically.

Climatic Diversity Equals Ecological Diversity

The Stein's remarkably diverse array of terrain and vegetation is a product of the different climatic conditions found throughout the watershed.

Glaciation

The large ice sheets that once covered much of the Stein were the most formative form of moisture the valley has been exposed to (see **Geology and Landforms**, p. 47). Since the glaciers receded about 10,000 years ago, downward erosion by water and gravity has kept the soils on the steep glaciated valley sides relatively thin and coarse. As a result, the vegetation here is sparse and scrubby, but nevertheless, it plays an important role in providing shelter and root systems, which slow further erosion.

In comparison, the flatter valley bottoms have been less exposed to the effects of erosion. Here, the soils have accumulated to greater depths and retained fertile fine soil particles. In addition, the milder valley-bottom climate allows for more biological activity and decomposition in the soil, enhancing soil fertility. Thus, the valley-bottom soils have produced plant communities that have greater biomass and more complex structures, which in turn support more plentiful and diverse animal populations.

One example of the impact of different geological processes on the vegetation cover is found in talus and avalanche slopes such as those shown here near the head of Nesbitt Creek. An examination of these areas shows that these processes produce different rates of soil development, which in turn influence the plants that are able to colonize these slopes. (J.R.)

Geography

As described in **Vegetation**, p. 52, the Stein's geographic location and mountainous terrain also contribute to its ecological diversity. The cool, moist Coast Mountains climate, which extends into the western end of the valley, has been most favourable for cedar, hemlock, and balsam forests with a dense undergrowth of blueberry and other shrubs. Conversely, the dry, warm climate of the eastern half of the Stein has resulted in sparse Douglas fir and pine forests with an open ground cover of grass and shrubs.

Similarly, from the Engelmann spruce - subalpine fir forests of the lower subalpine to the open heather meadows, herbs, and lichens of the alpine, a dramatic change in vegetation takes place as one moves up the mountain slopes. This transition reflects the increasingly longer winters and colder, moister weather associated with gains in elevation.

The River

The middle portion of the river is flat not only in cross-section due to the effects of past glaciation, but also in stream gradient, resulting in the river's meandering path. This in turn causes the river to sometimes change course during high water. The flooding river often cuts through sharp bends, leaving behind old unused sections of riverbed, and covers surrounding lowlands.

The resulting conditions have allowed a lush, predominantly deciduous forest ecosystem to develop in the otherwise dry conditions of the mid Stein. A common vegetation cover here is black cottonwood trees with a thick undergrowth of willow, both of which thrive in the moist conditions and rich silty soil laid down by countless floodwaters.

South facing slopes

Another climatic factor that greatly enhances ecological diversity in the Stein is the relative dryness of south and southwest facing slopes. These slopes' exposure to scorching summer sun results in summer drought conditions, which restricts plant growth and triggers frequent forest fires. As a result, the vegetation is often sparser on south and southwest facing slopes than on the north and northeast facing slopes. This pattern is common throughout the Stein, especially in the drier central and eastern portions of the valley.

Pileated woodpecker
(Pyrocopus pileatus)
This bird's large size (length: 40 cm) and distinct red crest (males) on the top of its head make it easy to identify. It can be found on dead or dying trees, logs, and stumps in search of carpenter ants. This old growth forest dependant woodpecker is commonly seen between the cable crossing and Scudamore Creek.(B.C. Parks)

Fires, Insects, and Disease

The Stein watershed has a long history of natural forest fires, insects, and disease, probably dating back to the first forests after the ice ages. These natural processes are absolutely essential for the overall health of the ecosystem.

Individual occurrences of fire, insects, and disease in the Stein have been limited in size, and uneven in shape and impact. These characteristics have encouraged healthy natural regeneration following the "disturbance," with the end result being a great enrichment of the natural patchwork of different aged forests, structures, and species throughout the Stein. Each kind of forest disturbance cannot spread very far before coming up against a different type of forest. Hence, this mosaic of different forest types is inherently resistant to large scale disturbances of any single kind - except logging, of course! A major ecological principle illustrated here is that "ecological diversity creates ecological resiliency and stability."

Animals

Each of the countless variants of terrain and vegetation described previously provide food and habitat requirements for a variety of animals during all or part of the year. Many of the interactions of these animals with their habitat environment and with each other have been studied under such scientific topics as "population dynamics," "food chains," and "trophic levels."

The Stein's diverse forest cover has helped to stop the numerous disturbances, such as fire, that regularly occur (W.C.W.C.)

The cavities created by the pileated woodpeckers in search of wood-boring insects are unmistakable. Eventually these cavities will be used by numerous other birds and mammals for nesting. (N.B.)

A few aspects of animal ecology are especially applicable here in the context of the watershed ecology of the Stein. These include some of the ways in which animals themselves sustain the health of the habitat they live in, and the dependance of many of the wildlife species on the precious intactness of the Stein valley for their survival.

Detritus feeders

The wheel of life in the Stein ecosystems can be said to begin with the many tiny animals and insects known as "detritus feeders" that work to decompose dead plant and animal matter. Thousands of species of microscopic mites and larger centipedes, worms, ants, beetles, fly larvae, and other insects chew up and excrete everything from dead leaves and needles to fallen logs and dead animals. Along with the action of bacteria, fungus, and chemical leaching by water, this decomposition releases nutrients for another cycle of absorption by plant communities, which in turn provides food and habitat for animals.

This is by far the most active level of the nutrient cycling pathways of an ecosystem. As much as 90 to 95% of the plant matter produced by perennial terrestrial plants is eventually consumed by detritus feeders, compared to only 5 to 10% by herbivores (plant-eating mammals). Despite this, much remains unknown about detritus feeders and nutrient cycling.

Rodents and forest regeneration

Recent research on the predominantly Douglas fir forests in Oregon and Washington has shown that small rodents such as the northern flying squirrel, deer mouse, and red-backed vole play a crucial role in the maintenance and regeneration of a forest ecosystem. It was discovered that rodents that feed on the fruiting bodies of underground fungus unknowingly distribute the fungus spores around the forest floor in their droppings (see **The Deer Mouse**, p.111, for more on the role of rodents in the forest ecosystem). These spores eventually germinate and extend fungal strands down to the root tips of coniferous trees.

The strands are important to the trees' health and growth, supplying roots with minerals, nutrients, nitrogen-fixing bacteria, and water (see **No Tree Should Be Without**, p. 109). The listed small rodent species all have British Columbia equivalents that live in the Stein valley, so it is very likely that these diminutive animals serve an equally crucial role in the maintenance and regeneration of the Stein forest ecosystem.

Wildlife Distribution

Both the detritus feeders and the small rodents described above stay within relatively defined areas throughout their lives. The detritus feeders are preyed upon by animals that are similarly confined in their movements such as spiders, sala-manders, and shrews. The small rodents, however, are preyed upon by weasel, marten, lynx, coyote, owl, and other larger carnivores and birds of prey that are broader ranging but whose numbers and distribution are not well known.

Larger animals in the Stein are known to follow migration routes to match their food and habitat requirements with the changing seasons. Their wide ranging movements make them especially vulnerable to the habitat disturbance and destruc-tion that would result from logging or road building anywhere in the watershed. Again, their exact numbers or distribution patterns have not been determined.

Mule deer, black bear, and mountain goat spend winters in or near the valley bottoms and move to higher elevations in the summer. The mid and lower Stein contain the relatively warm and dry lower levels of south facing slopes that are preferred winter habitat for all of the above species. The proposed road building and logging throughout this area would eliminate the forests that intercept snow, provide visual and thermal cover, and give escape routes from predators. Similarly, the forested North Stein valley is known grizzly habitat, yet the heavy logging proposed for this and the other valley bottom areas would almost undoubtedly eliminate this magnificent creature from the watershed.

Other wilderness-dependant wildlife species living in the Stein include human-avoiding species such as wolverine, lynx, cougar, and wolf. A large proportion of other wildlife species in the Stein are highly dependant on old-growth forests for their habitat needs, and include marten, pileated woodpecker, sala-manders, and possibly the elusive spotted owl (see **Mammals**, p. 68 and **Birds**, p. 62 for more information).

Streams

The Stein River itself supports both migratory and resident fish populations, important food sources for numerous carni-

Heart-leaf arnica
(Arnica cordifolia)
Found from valley bottom to subalpine, this 25-45 cm tall plant has yellow flowers and large, heart-shaped leaves. (B.C. Parks)

vores including black and grizzly bear. The flat meandering middle portion of the Stein provides especially important spawning and rearing habitat for numerous species (see **Fish**, p. 57, for a complete listing). This part of the Stein is extremely sensitive to damage by sedimentation and flash flooding, two possible side effects of road construction and logging.

Watershed Ecology

A new branch of ecology applicable to the Stein is watershed ecology. The word watershed refers to an area of the earth's surface where all the precipitation drains into a single watercourse. In this view, the Stein Valley is both a watershed comprised of smaller tributary watersheds, such as the Cottonwood and Scudamore valleys, and itself a tributary of the larger Fraser River watershed.

The key fact is that many of the connecting processes that weave the Stein together as a single ecological unit cross the boundaries of even the largest tributary watersheds. For example, the seeds of trees and other plants are transported throughout the Stein by wind and birds, connecting all areas in a single genetic mixing pool. Similarly, the seasonal movements of large wildlife species such as deer, bear, mountain goat, and cougar across the length and breadth of the Stein make these animals vulnerable to disturbances in any part of the watershed. The purity and stability of the mid and lower Stein River as spawning and rearing habitat for migratory and resident fish is dependant on the pristine intactness of the entire area drained by all the upstream tributaries.

Leaving the Stein in its natural state goes beyond simple wilderness preservation goals. As an intact watershed, it will also serve as a valuable classroom of nature's wonders. Its value as an intact wilderness watershed cannot be measured or even fully imagined, since we have barely even scratched the surface of understanding it.

GEOLOGY AND LANDFORMS

J. M. Ryder

The landforms of the Stein Valley reflect the erosion and deposition that have sculpted the present-day landscape out of the bedrock of the Coast Mountains. The effects of rock-forming processes, molten rock, glaciation, gravity, streams, and climate can be recognized and interpreted by any observant visitor.

Earth Materials

The bedrock of the Stein is typical of B.C.'s Coast Mountains. The widespread granitic rocks were formed by the cooling and crystallization of molten rock deep within the Earth's crust, about 50 million years ago. Since then, uplift and erosion have exposed these materials at the land surface. Granitic rocks are sufficiently coarse-grained that large, irregularly shaped crystals of quartz (glassy), feldspar (white), mica (shiny black or silver), hornblende (black), and chlorite (green) are clearly visible.

The great strength of the granitic rocks enables them to support very steep mountain-sides. Criss-crossing these rocks are joints (cracks) that tend to be farther apart than in other rocks. Consequently, blocks of granite that break free are very large, and their internal strength allows them to survive subsequent movement by ice and water. The bouldery nature of the terraces of the lower canyon is one result of this effect. Some major joints have been etched out by weathering or stream erosion to form deep clefts and gullies. Glacial erosion of granitic rock has produced rounded rock knobs and smooth cliffs with conspicuous sheeting joints (pseudo-layering).

The boulder-strewn terraces of the lower canyon (J.R.)

The toe of a rock glacier in a north-facing cirque at the head of Cottonwood Creek. (J.R.)

Small areas of the Stein basin are underlain by metamorphic, sedimentary, and volcanic rocks. Metamorphic (altered) rocks such as schist (a shiny, micaceous rock with a fine, sheet-like structure) occur throughout the basin. They were formed by the effects of heat and pressure on the original sedimentary rock into which the molten granite was intruded. Schist that contains crystals of garnet and staurolite (as well as mica) can be found on the ridges south of Scudamore Creek.

Sedimentary rocks, chiefly argillite and conglomerate (cemented mud and gravel respectively), underlie the most easterly three kilometres of the Stein Valley. These sediments accumulated in a marine environment, and were then displaced by faulting into their present position adjoining the granitic rocks. This north-south lying fault plane crosses the lower canyon.

Older schists and dark coloured ultramafic (iron and magnesium rich) rocks, which have been squeezed up from great depths, extend along the ridges and cirques between Doss Peak and Antimony, Skihist, and Petlushkwohap mountains. These rocks can be easily recognized from a distance by their dark and rusty red (when weathered) colours, and their tendency to disintegrate into very small fragments. Relatively young volcanic rocks are present in the western part of the Stein basin on some ridges, such as between Stein River and Rutledge Creek and between Cottonwood and Scudamore Creeks. They date from eruptions about 16 million years ago and can be distinguished by their columnar jointing (clearly-defined vertical cracks).

Shaping the Landscape

The most striking features of the Stein landscape are the landforms that were created by glacial erosion during the ice ages of the Pleistocene Epoch, 12,000 to 2 million years ago. The final cold period, known as Fraser Glaciation in B.C., started about 30,000 years ago when the climate began to deteriorate. Small snowfields in cirques gradually grew into long valley glaciers that eventually expanded out of the mountains and covered adjacent lowlands. At the height of the glaciation, about 14,500 years ago, the Stein basin was almost completely ice-covered. Only peaks higher than about 2600 m (8500 ft) protruded, forming barren, rocky islands in a vast, featureless snowfield. The ice sheet was short lived, however. Climatic warming resulted in rapid melting and glacier reces-

The well-defined, U-shaped North Stein is an excellent example of a glacially eroded trough (J.R.)

sion, so that by 11,000 years ago the valley was largely ice free and at least partly colonized by forest.

Most of the glacial landforms of the Stein basin remain relatively unscathed because they were chiselled into hard bedrock that has resisted the effects of subsequent weathering (rock disintegration and decomposition) and erosion. Today, all of the main valleys except the lower canyon have the characteristic U-shape of glacially eroded troughs. The floor of the main Stein River valley is now lower than the floors of its tributary valleys because the main valley was severely eroded by a large, fast-flowing glacier. Rapids and waterfalls mark the sites where these hanging tributaries join the main river. Steep-sided, bowl-shaped valley heads and shelf-like features on mountain walls are the cirques where the glaciers originated. Many of the alpine lakes occupy cirques: Cirque, Tundra, and Blowdown lakes are but a few of these. Stein Lake, in contrast, occupies a depression in a glacial trough.

The Finishing Touches

Today's small glaciers are not simply the shrunken remnants of Fraser Glaciation ice sheet. In fact, glaciers may not have existed here at all between 10,000 and 6000 years ago because the climate was warmer and drier then. Glaciers reappeared at the end of this period, and since then they have expanded and contracted several times in accordance with minor changes in the climate. Most recently, they began to expand about 1000 years ago, and continued to grow until the nineteenth century. At this time, they were larger than they had been at any time

Little Ice Age moraines of a receding glacier at the head of Kent Creek. (J.R.)

since Fraser Glaciation. This recent period of cool climate, known as "Little Ice Age," was a world wide phenomenon.

In the Stein basin, the extent of the Little Ice Age glaciers can be easily deduced from the position of the still incompletely vegetated end moraines (ridges of glacial debris) that lie beyond the modern shrunken glaciers. A few of the larger glaciers, such as the Rutledge, have extensive forefields of bare glacial soil that have been uncovered by recent glacier recession. In some forefields, closely spaced morainal ridges about a metre high mark the yearly positions of the receding glacier. Fine silt particles (rock flour) are formed by the glacial grinding of rocks and carried downstream in meltwater. These microscopic rock fragments remain suspended in the waters of alpine lakes where they refract blue light from the sky, giving the lakes their distinct colours.

Even though most of the rocks of the Stein basin are relatively resistant to weathering and the pull of gravity, downslope movement of rocky debris has occurred frequently during the past 11,000 years and still continues. Rockfalls occur when loose rock is released by ice melting in cracks and joints, resulting in talus slopes such as the Devil's Staircase. Some loosened rocks lodge temporarily in steep gullies, only to be washed out during heavy rains as debris flows, which contribute to the build up of debris fans on the valley floor. These fans are most easily identified in the lower canyon.

Major catastrophic rockslides have also shaped the landscape. For example Kent Lake and Devils Lake, are dammed by rockslides. The Devils Lake slide was so large that it travelled for several kilometres down Siwhe valley. Similarly, the huge granitic blocks that extend for more than a kilometre below "The Forks" of Stryen Creek are a rockslide. A comparatively small but recent rockslide has affected a steep slope on the south side of Stein River about two kilometres east of Ponderosa Creek.

Snow avalanches are frequent during winter and early spring in all but the lowest and most easterly parts of the basin. Active avalanche slopes below tree line are clearly marked by avalanche tracks of low, shrubby vegetation that appear as paler green stripes between darker swaths of mature forest. In the more snow-laden western areas, such as the North Stein, some avalanche tracks are so broad that they encompass entire mountainsides.

Not all gravitational processes result in the rapid falling or sliding of rocks. In areas above timberline, solifluction (slow downhill flow of soil) results in the formation of steep-fronted lobes and terraces of gravelly soil, a metre or two high. Rock glaciers (glacier-shaped masses of angular rock fragments which contain buried ice) are a much larger but equally slow-moving landform. Good examples exist on the north sides of Stein and Siwhe Mountains and smaller features can be found high on north-facing slopes.

Glacier meltwater, debris flows and slope wash provide silt, sand, gravel and boulders to the river and its tributaries. The sand and coarser materials are then transported downstream sporadically. Where stream gradients decrease or are gentle, these sediments are temporarily deposited, resulting in the formation of gravel bars, floodplains, and alluvial fans. During floods, sediment is remobilized by erosion and conveyed on the next leg of its journey. The mid-section of the Stein has a well-developed floodplain across which the river meanders irregularly. The channel constantly shifts its position because erosion occurs rapidly during high water on the outside banks of the meanders. The beaver pond between the lower cable crossing and Ponderosa Creek is one such meander that has been cut off from the main channel. Alluvial fans and debris flow fans are located where steep tributaries flow out onto the floodplain. The fans of Cottonwood and Ponderosa Creeks are two of the more obvious alluvial fans encountered when hiking in the valley.

The Valley Today and Tomorrow

Millions of years of Earth history are represented in the physical landscape of the Stein. Its rocks and landforms are the result of an interweaving of processes generated by both the Earth and the atmosphere. Glaciers etched out the major features of the valley, and when the ice melted, glacial soils were rapidly colonized by vegetation. Now, the forest and the alpine tundra are ruptured only occasionally by falling rocks and floods of debris, while ice is confined to remote heights. Within the span of geological time, however, evolution of the landscape will continue inevitably. Will warm Ponderosa-pine covered slopes predominate, or do the glaciers on the valley's rim have another major role in the future?

The large alluvial fan of Ponderosa Creek is apparent from most vantage points. (J.R.)

VEGETATION

Introduction

The Stein Valley's diverse vegetation reflects the pronounced differences in precipitation that occur throughout the watershed. The cool, wet Coast Mountain peaks on the western boundaries of the Stein collect much of the moisture from passing Pacific storms, forming a strong rain shadow effect eastwards towards the Fraser River. Whereas annual precipitation in the headwaters west of Stein Lake is about 200 cm, the lower Stein receives only 45 cm of precipitation per year.

In classifying the different ecosystems of B.C., ecologists have identified 12 climatically distinct zones. These biogeoclimatic or ecological zones are differentiated by distinct patterns of vegetation and soil, and are usually named after the climax tree species which dominate the ecosystem. Under this system, the Stein's diversity is apparent; no less than six different zones are found within the Stein. For ease of use, the following section is broken into more easily identified areas within the Stein watershed.

The River Mouth

The rain shadow's effect is most evident at the eastern end of the valley, especially near the mouth of the river. Ponderosa pine, a species typical of hot, arid areas, dominates the forested benches surrounding the river mouth. Douglas fir is also present, but it is not as common as further west in the valley. This generally open forest has abundant shrubs and grasses growing on rocky soil between sparse trees. This is the Ponderosa Pine - Bunchgrass (PPBG) zone, the hottest and driest zone in B.C. Unfortunately, the lower Stein is one of the few relatively undisturbed dry belt areas left in B.C.

Some of the more common shrubs found here include Saskatoon berry, rabbitbrush, ceanothus (two species), sagebrush, and Oregon grape. Clumps of blue-bunch wheatgrass, one of the original grasses now rare due to overgrazing, roadbuilding, and cultivation, are found on some steep enbankments. Cheatgrass and knapweed are much more common.

The pine tree-dominated alluvial fan of the Stein-Fraser rivers confluence (A.B.)

The Lower Canyon

Ponderosa Pine/Fir Forest

The first few kilometres of the main trail pass through mixed forests of Ponderosa and lodgepole pine, and Douglas fir. Ponderosa pine is predominant on steep, rocky areas, especially on south facing slopes. These trees, in fact, occur in dry sites as far west as Stein Lake. Douglas fir is more prevalent on north-facing slopes and on areas that are shaded and moister. As one moves further west, Douglas fir becomes the dominant tree cover in this, the largest and most diverse ecological zone in the Stein, the Interior Douglas Fir (IDF) zone.

Shrubbery and flowers

Shrubs found in the lower canyon include Oregon grape, kinnikinnik, soopalalie (soapberry), Douglas maple, ceanothus, Saskatoon berry, and birch-leaved spirea. Wildflowers blossom in the lower canyon from late April to early June. Sage buttercup, yellow bell, larkspur, and shrubby penstemon appear first. Later there are chocolate lily, death camas, silky lupine, balsamroot, paintbrush, alum root, gromwell, three-flowered avens, and both rosy and dwarf pussytoes. From late June through July you may find mariposa lily, heart-leaved arnica, yarrow, salsify, brown-eyed Susan, slender hawk's beard, hawkweed, sand goldenrod, white thistle, and dogbane. Rabbitbrush flowers latest, from September into October.

Covering the tree trunks, branches, and boulders of the lower canyon are lichens of numerous textures and colours. From the Trailhead to "Devil's Staircase," the colourful yellowish-green wolf lichen (*Letharia vulpina*) is strikingly evident. (See **Divorce is out of the Question**, p. 160, for more information on lichens.)

Cedar Groves

The diversity of the Stein's forests is evident in the eastern reaches of the valley. Situated along the creeks that cross the dry, hot benches next to the Stein are the cool, moist cedar groves of Stryen, Teaspoon, and Earl Creeks. Such cedar stands are rare in the rain shadow east of the Coast divide. These pockets of western red cedar are important to the valley's diverse wildlife, and become more common as one travels westward into the watershed. Cedar was used extensively by the native peoples, as evidenced by the number of

Oregon grape
(*Berberis repens*)
This low-lying shrub's distinctive evegreen, holly-like leaves distinguish it from other plants also found in open forests. (N.B.)

One bear's signature on the trunk of an aspen (*Populus tremuloides*). (N.B.)

culturally modified trees (CMTs). See **Making Use of the Parts**, p. 100 for more information on the Indian uses of cedar roots and bark.

The Mid-Valley

The Interior Douglas-fir zone extends throughout the mid-valley of the Stein, where the forest composition varies greatly. Douglas fir, the dominant species, is found on much of the lower elevation slopes and benches alongside the river. It is also predominant along the lower and middle reaches of tributary valleys. Lodgepole pine is common in the mid-valley, especially on the dry ridges of the main valley's slopes.

Occurring less frequently are aspen, which tends to be scattered amongst tall conifers, and western yew, a deciduous tree that grows slowly under the Douglas fir canopy. The occasional birch may be found in mixed groves. On moister sites, western white pine and western red cedar appear, becoming more common as one travels farther up the Stein. Engelmann spruce also occurs fairly frequently, especially upriver, on major upper Stein tributaries and on northern exposures.

These mixed forests serve as travel corridors for wildlife, and are important winter habitat for animals as only small amounts of snow ever carpet their floors. Unfortunately, this forest is vastly under-represented in our parks system, as it is one of the forest industry's principal timber supplies.

Many different shrubs and herbs grow in the rich central valley forests. Shrubs found here include common juniper, Oregon grape, Douglas maple, Sitka mountain-ash, soopalalie, Saskatoon berry, huckleberry, thimbleberry, snowberry, chokecherry, redstem ceanothus, kinnikinnik, falsebox, ocean spray, and western trumpet honeysuckle. In the drier eastern valley forests pinegrass dominates the ground cover, often accompanied by yarrow, aster, wild strawberry, pussytoe, and twinflower. Further west, moister conditions promote mosses and herbs such as twisted stalk and foamflower. Also present are rattlesnake plantain, star-flowered Solomon's seal, false sarsaparilla, vanilla leaf, bunchberry, and wintergreen.

Floodplain Cottonwood Forests

From the cable crossing to Nesbitt Creek, floodplain forests have developed where flooding regularly occurs. Deciduous trees such as northern black cottonwood (see **The Cotton-**

wood, p. 105 for more information), birch, western red cedar, and mountain alder dominate these vegetation communities, which contrast sharply with their neighbouring conifers. On less frequently flooded terraces, a mixed forest of Douglas fir, cottonwood, aspen, western white pine, and Engelmann spruce appears. Shrubs tend to be dense and tall in these forests, as best exemplified by willow thickets. In addition to several species of willow, red osier dogwood, beaked hazelnut, thimbleberry, wild rose, black twinberry, snowberry, Saskatoon berry, and birch leafed spirea are also present.

The Upper Valley

In the western regions of the valley where moisture is abundant, forests become more "coastal" in character. Here, the dense canopy and moss carpeted forest floor of the Coastal Western Hemlock (CWH) zone is apparent. This zone is characterized by mixed stands of hemlock, cedar, spruce, and fir. In the North Stein and Rutledge systems and along the upper Stein River below Stein Lake, pockets of Pacific silver fir, western hemlock, and amabilis fir appear in moist areas. Such stands of original forest are now becoming rare in B.C.

Subalpine Forests

The subalpine is a transition zone between the denser, lower elevation forests and the barren, higher elevation alpine. Here, elevation has a major effect on factors such as average temperature, moisture availability, and wind exposure, all of which change significantly as you move from the valley floor to the mountain peaks.

Above the valley bottom forests, more sparsely forested Engelmann spruce and subalpine fir forests predominate. These are the Montane Spruce (MS) and Engelmann Spruce - Subalpine fir (ESSF) zones. Lodgepole pine, amabilis fir, the occasional Douglas fir, and even western hemlock may also be found here. On drier and warmer slopes to the north and east, lodgepole pine and whitebark pine are quite common, while amabilis fir, Douglas fir and even western hemlock occur in the western regions of the Stein.

Subalpine Parkland

As you climb higher, the subalpine forest thins out into subalpine parkland - an attractive mosaic of tree clumps and open heath or herb meadows. In the upper western Stein where

Bracken fern
(*Pteridium aquilinum pubescens*)
The most common fern in B.C., the bracken fern is found in lower elevation coniferous forests. (R.B.C.M.)

the climate is moister, subalpine fir is the most common parkland tree. Engelmann spruce is a fairly frequent associate and mountain hemlock is occasional. In the drier mountains towards the east there is no mountain hemlock. Subalpine fir, though still frequent, decreases and Engelmann spruce and whitebark pine predominate. Shrubs tend to cluster around tree clumps. Open meadowland is primarily heath in the west, herb meadows in the east.

Alpine

The Alpine Tundra (AT) zone begins at treeline, which occurs between 1620 m (5400 ft.) and 1890 m (6300 ft.) in the Stein. The severe environmental conditions of this zone limit the vegetation types to a few specialized species. Trees are limited in their growth and size, resulting in stunted - less than a metre in height - and twisted shrubs known as krummholz (German for "bent wood"). Krummholz tree species include Engelmann spruce, subalpine fir, and whitebark pine. Mountain hemlock is found in higher snowfall areas. Step carefully around these trees; one branch may take up to 50 years to grow, with some trees growing for hundreds of years.

Several types of vegetation cover exist in the subalpine and alpine. Heather meadows (heaths) are the most common in the higher snowfall reaches of the Stein. A soft carpet of evergreen dwarf shrubs, especially the white, red, and yellow heathers, rowberry, and low blueberries predominate in these meadows.

At the edge of tarns, along the banks of alpine streams, and in deep snowbed areas in depressions, sedge marsh vegetation is prevalent. In snow patch areas, sedges are well established. Alongside streams, blackheaded sedge, willow thickets, and numerous flowers occur. On slopes that are more moderate, moister, and that have deeper soils, alpine flowers such as avalanche lilies, western anemone, and spring beauty appear.

Low-lying plants and colourful lichens are most common in the true alpine areas, which are dry, relatively snow-free exposed ridges. On boulder-strewn slopes with relatively barren, gravelly soiled slopes, only crevices and moist, textured soil are inhabited by plants. Rock surfaces that do not receive large snow accumulations are covered by lichens such as the green map lichen (*rhizocarpon geographicum*), the distinctly orange xanthoria lichen, umbilicaria genus lichens, and crustose lichens.

FISH

Murray Lashmar

Introduction

Six fish species, all members of the salmonid family, live in the Stein River Valley: Rainbow or Steelhead trout, Dolly Varden char, mountain whitefish, and pink, coho, and chinook salmon. Other species may be present. The same quality that makes the Stein attractive as a wilderness area - its remoteness - also limits what is known about its fish populations.

The spawning season is probably the best time for fish watching. To observe fish, you may want to wear polarizing sunglasses, which reduce the glare off the water. Also, be sure to move slowly near the water to avoid disturbing the fish.

History

Salmonids re-entered the Stein River after the glaciers of the last ice age receded 10,000 years ago. From ice-free areas in the lower Columbia River, they followed the retreating ice northward into B.C. Reaching the headwaters of the Columbia, the salmonids crossed into the Fraser River drainage through a series of glacial meltwater lakes lying between Golden and Valemount. From the upper Fraser, they moved downstream to the Stein. In contrast, pink salmon reached the Stein from the west coast after the ice which was blocking the lower Fraser melted.

Life History

Trout, salmon, char, and whitefish begin their life cycle as fertilized eggs deposited on or under the surface of the streambed. Oxygen-rich waters flow through the gravel, supplying the eggs with nutrients necessary for growth. The eggs hatch, producing alevins, young fish with an attached yolk sac or food supply. After the alevins have consumed the yolk, they emerge as free-swimming fry from the shelter of the stream bottom to feed on insect larvae such as mayflies, stoneflies, and caddisflies, and crustaceans such as amphipods and freshwater shrimp.

Developing salmonids, eggs and alevins, in particular, are very vulnerable to changes in streamflow, water quality, temperature, and siltation. Fry also have a tough time of it - fewer than ten percent survive past the first few months, the victims of predation and competition.

The surviving fry either remain in freshwater permanently (rainbow, mountain white-fish, and Dolly Varden char), or spend up to two years in freshwater before migrating downstream to the ocean for one to five years (steelhead and salmon) and then returning to their freshwater spawning grounds. Those species which mature in saltwater before returning to freshwater to spawn are termed anadromous. Biologists believe that salmonids evolved in freshwater and later adapted to saltwater after being in the ocean during the ice ages

In the ocean, salmon and steelhead grow rapidly, feeding initially on small prey such as shrimp, and later on, larger fish such as sandlance and herring. Before returning to freshwater, they may travel up to 3000 kilometres across the Pacific Ocean.

While all salmonids migrate to their spawning grounds, anadromous fish undertake the most dramatic journey. Guided in the open ocean by the position of the sun, they swim towards the mouth of the Fraser River until they are able to detect the unique chemical smell of their home stream. Entering the Fraser, they continue upriver, ignoring streams lacking this "fingerprint" until they finally reach the Stein. Salmon spawning in other rivers such as in the upper Fraser may migrate upriver 1000 km further. Amazingly, spawning fish complete their entire journey without eating. They rely totally on energy reserves of protein and fat stored during their last months at sea.

After finding the stream where they were born, members of the salmonid family search for well-aerated, even-sized stream gravel. Males and females pair up, quiver, and simultaneously release eggs and sperm directly onto the stream bottom or into redds (depressions) excavated by the female. They continue spawning until all eggs and sperm are released.

Eggs are fertilized immediately and settle into crevices in the gravel or are covered over again in the redd by the female. The redds can sometimes be seen as lighter areas in the stream bottom where the overlying rocks have been removed. Spawning completed and their energy spent, anadromous spawners usually die within one or two days after spawning, although coho salmon may live for several more weeks. Freshwater species, on the other hand, may survive to spawn several years in a row. And so the cycle begins again.

Fish Habitat and Distribution

The main Stein can be divided into three sections: The lower canyon, the mid-Stein, and the upper Stein. Each area differs from the others in the fish species present and opportunities for watching fish.

Between the mouth and the lower canyon, where the river cuts through the terraces of the Fraser River, look for pink salmon spawning. At the mouth itself, non-salmonids such as peamonth chub, northern squawfish, longnose and leopard dace may be seen. Above the terraces, the river squeezes through the steep-sided lower canyon. There, large boulders

Stonefly nymph
(Order Plecoptera)
Found on the bottom of streams and well-aerated lakes. This yellowish or brown 40 mm long larvae has two distinct sensory organs projecting from its rear end. Feeds on vegetation, but is sometimes omnivorous. May live up to three years before leaving the water to begin the adult part of its cycle. (B.C. Parks)

and steep gradients make spawning highly unlikely. Deep pools and still water behind boulders enable adults and young fish to rest during their travels.

In the mid Stein between Earl and Nesbitt Creeks, the river meanders through the wide valley. Excellent spawning grounds of well-aerated, uniform gravel for all species except pinks (which are probably stopped by the lower canyon) are found here. Each year, small runs (less than 100 fish each) of steelhead, coho, and chinook migrate to this part of the river to spawn.

The mid Stein also contains high quality nursery areas for young fish. Riffles of rocks and gravel provide a source of aquatic insect larvae, the most common fish food. The larvae graze over the rocks, eating algae and small prey. When tired, young fish rest in the numerous side channels, pools, and quiet waters behind boulders.

Look for coho fry under well-vegetated streambanks or in pools. Steelhead, on the other hand, prefer riffles and boulder areas. Dolly Varden are the only fish seen in Scudamore Creek, a tributary of the Stein. The presence of Longnose and largescale suckers there has not been confirmed, but the habitat is suitable for these species.

Above Nesbitt Creek, the river straightens and steepens, and the riverbed gravel becomes larger, producing conditions more conducive to rearing fry. 42 km from the Fraser River, a five metre high waterfall blocks upstream movement to all but flying fish.

Between the waterfall and Stein Lake, only rainbow trout live. No one knows for sure how they got there. Perhaps an early pioneer carried them over the falls to ensure a food source. Or perhaps the rainbow become isolated when an earthquake raised the barrier. In any event, no fish have been seen either in Stein Lake or in the headwater lakes above Stein Lake. Unlike many areas in B.C., this area has not been stocked, probably because of its remoteness.

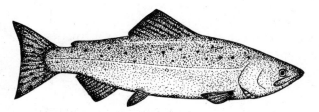

Pink salmon (*Oncorhynchus gorbuscha*) (B.C. Parks)

Barred owl
(Strix varia)
An occasional consumer of fish, the barred owl is more likely to pursue rodents, birds, and insects. This commonly heard but less frequently seen owl can be identified by its hornless head, large barred ruff below its bill, and a streaked front. (R.B.C.M.)

Fish of the Stein

Anadromous

Pink Salmon (*Oncorhynchus gorbuscha*)

Pink salmon, the smallest of the Pacific salmon, spawn in late summer or early fall, their fertilized eggs developing and hatching under the cover of winter. The fry emerge from the gravel in the spring and migrate immediately to the sea. They spend two to three months in estuaries and nearshore waters, feeding and adapting to the saltwater environment before migrating farther offshore. In the autumn of the following year, at two years of age, they return to spawn.

Pinks spawn each year in the Stein, but because of the two year cycle, heavy runs in odd-numbered years (e.g., 1991) alternate with light runs in even-numbered years. In the 1980s, approximately 2000 pink salmon per odd year spawned compared to about 200 per year in the 1960s.

Coho Salmon (*Oncorhynchus kisutch*)

Rivers swollen by autumn rains provide coho salmon with the water volume needed to migrate upstream to their spawning grounds. Several weeks later they spawn, leaving their fertilized eggs to mature over the winter. Fry emerge from the gravel the following spring to feed on larval and adult insects. Coho are very territorial, defending their feeding areas aggressively. They stay in fresh water one to two years, then migrate seaward to grow for two more years, feeding on the abundant microscopic animals. Coho mature sexually after three to four years.

Chinook Salmon (*Oncorhynchus tshawytscha*)

The largest of the Pacific salmon, chinook spawn between September and November. Where spawning grounds are far from the ocean, they begin migrating as early as May. Chinook fry emerge in the spring, and spend two to twelve months in fresh water. Not as aggressive as coho, chinook gather in schools briefly before dispersing to form territories. They mature after three to five years in salt water.

Steelhead Trout (*Salmo gairdneri*)

Steelhead trout, the anadromous form of rainbow trout, migrate in late summer to early fall. Unlike salmon, but like freshwater salmonids, steelhead feed during migration. Steelheads spawn in late winter or early spring as water temperatures rise. Eggs incubate during the spring and fry emerge into the streams in June or July. Juvenile steelhead remain in fresh water for two to three years before moving to saltwater for a further two to three years of growth. They are ready to spawn at four to six years of age. A small number, usually females, migrate downstream again to the ocean and then return the following year to spawn a second time.

Resident

Rainbow Trout (*Salmo gairdneri*)

Rising spring or summer water temperatures stimulate rainbow trout to spawn in fine gravel riffles (shallow, fast moving areas with rocky or gravelly bottoms) above a pool. Four to eight weeks later, the fry emerge to feed on larval and adult insects, leeches, molluscs (e.g., freshwater snails), and small fish. Adults add larger insects and crustaceans to their diet, and mature in three to four years. Rainbow normally spawn once in their lifetime, but have been known to spawn up to five times.

Mountain Whitefish (*Prosopium williamsoni*)

On late fall or early winter nights, mountain whitefish lay their eggs and sperm (or milt) directly on the stream bottom rather than in a redd or nest. The fertilized eggs hatch in March or April. Fry emerge to feed along the stream bottom on aquatic insect larvae, fish eggs, and as they mature, occasional adult insects. Mountain whitefish fry may protect themselves by forming large schools instead of hiding under rocks. They mature at three years of age.

Dolly Varden char (*Salvelinus malma*)

September brings spawning Dolly Varden char to stream sections with medium to large sized gravel beds and moderate currents. Males are extremely aggressive, driving off competing males. Females may be accompanied by several males, but only one will dominate. Eggs and alevins develop during the winter and fry leave the gravel by late April to mid-May. Feeding on larval and adult insects, snails, and leeches, the young fish grow rapidly. As adults, Dolly Varden feed on bottom-dwelling organisms, salmonid eggs, fry, and small trout. By late summer, Dollies move into headwater and tributaries. At five years of age, they are ready to spawn.

BIRDS

Jennifer Nener

The Stein's diverse landscape supports a tremendous variety of birds. The following focuses on the appearance, habitat, and behaviour of 16 birds commonly seen in the Stein.

Raptorial Birds

Raptors can be loosely defined as "birds of prey." These flesh-eating birds have a strong, hooked beak, and four well-developed toes, each endowed with a sharp claw or talon for seizing prey.

Sharp shinned hawk (*Accipiter striatus velox*)

The 35 cm long sharp shinned hawk has a 60 cm wingspan and is identified by its horizontally barred, reddish breast, blue-grey back and upper wing feathers, black crown, and red eyes. It is also distinguished by its short, rounded wings and square-tipped tail, which has a slight notch when folded. The similar but larger Cooper's hawk, which is occasionally sighted in the Stein, has a long, rounded tail. In mid-mountain country look for the sharp shinned hawk gracefully threading its way through the trees at low levels, in pursuit of small birds such as kinglets, sparrows, and towhees. Its diet is supplemented by lizards, insects, and small mammals.

Merlin (*Falco columbarius columbarius*)

Previously known as the Pigeon hawk, the merlin is one of the smallest falcons (length 30 cm, wingspan 58 cm). It is endowed with grey-blue plumage above and brown below. Black bands on the tail help one to avoid confusing this bird with the similar but larger peregrine falcon; pointed wings distinguish it from the sharp shinned hawk. The merlin can be found over open fields, moorlands, and short grass benches near the mouth of the Stein River. Unlike other raptors it does not swoop or soar. Instead it hunts at tree-top level, capturing small birds in mid-air. Insects, bats, and other small mammals are also consumed.

Barred owl (*Strix varia*)

This large (length 43 cm, wingspan 112 cm) hornless owl is identified by its grey-brown colour and vertically streaked front. Like the northern spotted owl, this species prefers to live in old growth forest near rivers. Small rodents such as mice and voles, and less often birds, insects, frogs, and fish, make up its diet. The barred owl may be responsible for the possible extirpation of the spotted owl from the valley. Its only known predator is the great horned owl.

Ground-dwelling Birds

These are typically well camouflaged chicken-like birds which feed on insects, seeds, berries, and whatever else they can peck from the ground and low shrubs.

Ruffed grouse (*Bonasa umbellus sabini*)

The forest floor dwelling ruffed grouse is easily distinguished from other species by its crested head and broad, barred tail. This species occurs in two colour phases: Red birds with rufous tails, and grey-brown birds with grey tails. Males have a red spot above the eye. From March until May, the slow "thump, thump, thump" mating call can be heard for a half a kilometre but is not easily located.

Blue grouse (Sooty Grouse)
(*Dendragapus obscurus fuliginosus*)

At a length of 43 cm, this is the largest species of grouse to inhabit the Stein. Males have dark breasts, instead of the mottled brown and white breasts characteristic of other species, and also feature a yellow spot above the eye. Females are grey-brown, barred with black. Both sexes sport a black tail with a grey band at the end. The blue grouse is common in subalpine-fir forest close to timberline. Blue grouse will freeze upon approach, relying on their camouflage to keep them safe. Like other grouse, they take wing under a loud flurry of noise if approached too closely. Inflated throat sacs are the source of the ventriloquist voice of the blue grouse, which can be heard for several kilometres.

Pygmy owl
(*Glaucidium gnoma*)
The smallest of the owls in B.C., measuring only 15 cm in length with a wingspan of 40 cm. This tiny owl is mostly active at dawn and dusk in pursuit of rodents, small birds, and insects. (R.B.C.M.)

White-tailed ptarmigan (*Lagopus leucurus*)

Ptarmigan plumage changes with the seasons in order to provide year-round camouflage. In the summer this species is mottled brown and white, with white breast, wings, and tail. In the winter, individuals are pure white except for a black beak and eyes. With a length of only 25 cm, ptarmigan are substantially smaller than grouse and have feathers on their feet, which grouse lack. The white-tailed ptarmigan has been described as fearless, and perhaps more accurately as somewhat daft, as it may march right over the front of your hiking boots if you keep still enough!

Warblers

Numerous species of warblers are commonly found in the Stein. They are generally active little birds, usually smaller than sparrows. Warblers often have some yellow pigmentation, and characteristically have narrow, pointed beaks. They are about 12 cm in length.

Yellow-rumped warbler (*Dendroica coronata auduboni*)

Previously known as Audubon's Warbler, this bird is one of the most common warblers in the Stein. It is one of the few warblers seen throughout the year. The bright yellow rump, crown, and side patches together with a white tail patch are the primary markings of this species. Both the Audubon's race, which has a yellow throat, and the Myrtle race, which has a white throat, occur in the Stein. These were originally considered to be two separate species.

The agile yellow-rumped warbler is often seen bursting from tree tops in pursuit of insects, zig-zagging as skillfully as a flycatcher. Look for it hunting among firs, pines, and, less frequently, willows. During breeding season it is found at higher elevations.

Townsend's warbler *(Dendroica townsendi)*

Identified by its dark crown, yellow breast, and dark ear patch bordered by yellow, the Townsend's warbler is a difficult bird to detect since it spends most of its time near the tops of tall fir and spruce trees. Exhibiting typical warbler behavior, it flies nervously out from a high perch in pursuit of insects, less frequently supplementing its diet with fruits and nectar.

Wilson's warbler (*Wilsonia pusilla chryseola*)

Undoubtedly one of the prettiest warblers in the west, with its olive upper, bright yellow lower body, and distinctive small black cap (male). Wilson's warbler is found in willow marshes or similar thickets near streams, on avalanche slopes, and amidst scrubby coniferous growth. This brightly coloured bird can be observed moving about the shrubbery, gleaning insects off the branches and out of the air. When perching, the Wilson's warbler may twitch its tail up and down intermittently while emitting its fluctuating thin and rapid chatter.

Chickadees (Parus species)

Chickadees are rotund little birds (length 11 cm) with long tails and no neck. They have disproportionately large heads and small beaks. The unmistakable bib and black cap, white cheek patches, and characteristic "chick-a-dee-dee-dee" call will easily distinguish the small black-capped chickadee from others. It also lacks rufous on the back and flanks, allowing one to distinguish this species from the chestnut-backed chickadee.

Pine siskin
(*Carduelis pinus*)
This small (12 cm long) finch is very common in forests, normally travelling in flocks above the forest canopy. The upper body is greyish-brown with darker streaking while the wings and tail are edged in white or pale yellow. (R.B.C.M.)

The mountain chickadee sports a white eyebrow stripe, and has a white breast with grey sides. The somewhat rare boreal chickadee has a brown cap and a white breast with cinnamon coloured sides, in contrast to the plain grey breast of the black-capped chickadee. Insects and insect eggs and larvae are primary components of their diet, although they also feed on seeds and fruit. Chickadees are often observed hanging upside down as they forage amongst the conifers and mixed woods, or flying through the trees in small, irrepressibly cheerful groups.

Nuthatches (Sitta species)

Nuthatches are small, stubby birds. They are distinguished from the chickadees by their lack of a black bib and relatively large beaks, which are similar in form to the beak of a woodpecker. The white-breasted nuthatch is the largest species of nuthatch found in the Stein (length 13 - 15 cm). The back is slate-blue, while the crown, hindneck, and shoulders are shiny black. As you might guess from the name, its breast is pure white, as are its cheeks.

Black- capped chickadee
(*Parus atricapillus*)
This very common chickadee is often found in conifers and mixed woods searching for insects, larvae, and seeds.(R.B.C.M.)

The red-breasted nuthatch is about 11 cm long. This black-capped, white throated, rusty bellied resident of semi-open Ponderosa pine forest near mid-mountain range is easily identified. Like other nuthatches the back is slate-blue. However, it is the only species of nuthatch having a broad black line through the eye and a white line above it. The pygmy nuthatch is the smallest of the nuthatches in the Stein (length 10 cm). Like the other species it is slate-blue on the back; however, the crown is greyish-brown to olive-grey instead of black and it has a white spot on the nape. Below, it is creamy white with grey flanks. Its cheeks are white, and a dark bar runs through the eye, blending into the crown without any light eyebrow streak in between.

Nuthatches are the only tree-climbers which habitually go down trees head first. They also travel upwards, forwards, backwards, and sometimes even creep along the underside of branches, in search of beetles and other creepy-crawlies. This contrasts with their frequent companion, the brown creeper, which gleans up a tree trunk and then flies to the low end of another trunk to start the process again. Nuthatches use their long, narrow bills to probe out protein-rich tree-dwelling insects, an important supplement to their primarily coniferous seed diet. The name nuthatch comes from nut-hack, which refers to their habit of placing a conifer cone in the furrows of a tree and hammering it apart with their bill.

Kinglets

Golden- crowned kinglet (*Regulus satrapa olivaceus*)

Regulus means "little king," a reference to its bright yellow head crown, bordered with black. Kinglets are olive-grey, and smaller than most warblers (about 9 - 10 cm in length). The male has a red stripe down the middle of the crown; the female is yellow only. Also useful in identification are the tiny, plump build, and long white stripe above the eye, which distinguish it from the golden crowned sparrow. Flocks are common in spruce and fir forest below 1350 m (4500 ft). These insectivorous birds can be seen moving quickly through the middle and upper conifer branches, gleaning and twittering merrily as they go. During the winter and into spring, one may find kinglets in a mixed flock of chickadees, brown creepers, nuthatches, and small woodpeckers.

Golden-crowned kinglet and **ruby-crowned kinglet**

(*Regulus satrapa* and *Regulus calendula*) Frequently seen in trees and shrubbery, these active little birds can be confused with other small birds. Their colourful crowns are key to proper identification. (R.B.C.M.)

Ruby- crowned kinglet (*Regulus calendula*)

This busy little bird is similar in appearance and habit to the golden- crowned kinglet, however it lacks both the eye-stripe and the bright yellow cap. Males have a scarlet crown, visible only when the bird is excited, while the females lack any conspicuous crown patch. The ruby crowned kinglet flits through the lower boughs of coniferous trees in search of insects, usually hunting singly or in pairs.

Other Birds

Pine grosbeak (*Pinicola enucleator*)

A large (length 20 cm), plump, long-tailed bird with a dark bill. The male has a red back, breast, and head, interspersed with patches of grey. The female is grey, brown, and variable yellow. This bird may be identified in the air by its undulating flight, and can be distinguished from the evening grosbeak by its long tail. The pine grosbeak is commonly observed in small flocks in coniferous forests at subalpine elevations in the warmer months, moving to lower elevations for the winter. An opportunistic feeder, the pine grosbeak consumes buds, fruit, and seeds of coniferous and deciduous trees.

Pileated woodpecker (*Dryocopus pileatus*)

North America's largest woodpecker (length 38 cm) is identified by its solid black back, white chin, red cap, and white under-wing pattern (seen only in flight). The presence of a large crest, red on the male and black on the female, is a further identifying feature. Like all woodpeckers, it has a long, stiff tail which it uses to brace itself while climbing. You will hear the familiar loud hammering of this bird as it chisels away at dead trees in the mixed forest of the mid valley region in search of bugs, which are extracted with its long and sticky tongue. Hammering also serves as a mode of communication and territorial defence. The pileated's rectangular-shaped nest and holes are easily differentiated from those of other woodpeckers, which tend be more square. Insects, fruits, acorns, and sap are its major food sources.

Rufous hummingbird (*Selasphorous rufus*)

This tiny species (7.5 cm length) is actually a relative of the woodpeckers. The adult male has a reddish-brown back, green crown, brilliant iridescent orange-red throat, and a white breast. Females are predominately green on the dorsal side, with some rufous at the base of the tail. The rufous hummingbird is normally found in coniferous forests, amidst flowering shrubs which yield red or yellow blossoms. Nectar, which it laps from flowers with its long tongue, and tree sap, which is obtained from woodpecker holes, provide sugar - the most important component of a hummer's diet. Protein is obtained from spiders and small insects.

Listen for the humming sound of the rufous' wings as it swoops by at speeds of up to 80 km/hour! Watch for the spectacular courtship display of the males in spring and early summer as they dive-bomb from a height of 15 m or more, and swerve upwards again at the last possible second, with the hope of impressing a near-by female!

Common nighthawk
(*Chordeiles minor hesperis*)
Look for this dark-coloured bird at dusk in pursuit of flying insects.
(R.B.C.M.)

MAMMALS

A large part of what makes the Stein so special is its inhabitants. Only three hours from a major metropolitan city, this intact ecosystem is home to over 50 mammalian species including cougar, grizzly bear, and wolverine. The presence of these large carnivores is especially significant because they depend on healthy populations of other mammals, birds, and fish. The following is an overview of some of the more common mammals in the Stein.

Shrews

What appears to be a mouse with a long pointed nose and thin tail is probably a shrew. Most species are about 10 cm long, including a 4 cm tail. This active little creature is actually an insectivore, which eats at least its own weight in food each day. The four different species of shrews found in the Stein's forests and meadows are often heard at night as you lie in your tent. The rustling of leaves and grass suggests a shrew is close by, seeking out insects, slugs, snails, spiders, fungi, and seeds. In winter, the shrews continue to seek out food, using tunnels built in air pockets of snow.

Bats

At least seven different members of the bat family live in the Stein. From the valley bottom (Stein Lake logjam and many of the major creeks such as Ponderosa, Cottonwood, and Scudamore are very active places in the early hours of the evening) to timberline, these nocturnal, airborne mammals are perpetually hunting flying insects, especially mosquitoes. Living in colonies, bats roost during the daytime in caves, rock overhangs, and tree hollows. Some hibernate during the winter, living off accumulated fat layers, while others migrate south (see **Winging It**, p. 118).

Snowshoe hare

Found primarily in wooded areas, the nocturnal snowshoe hare - the name comes from its large feet - feeds on wildflowers, grasses, and leaves in summer, buds, twigs, bark, and leaves of year-round green plants in winter. In summer, it is brown or grey with a white tummy, turning white with black tipped ears in winter. Snowshoe hare average 50 cm in length, including a 5 cm tail. A high reproductive rate allows the snowshoe hare to maintain its population since it is continually pursued by weasels, coyote, wolf, lynx, bobcat, and cougar. With a yearly survival rate of between 10 - 50 %, a snowshoe hare's life is not envious.

Pika

Heard, but not often seen as they lay perfectly still or hide between the rocks of their home, pikas are a fixture of boulder-strewn alpine slopes. Stacks of grasses, alpine wildflowers, sedges, and other alpine vegetation laid out on boulders to dry indicate the presence of these guinea-pig-like "rock rabbits." Pikas are grey-brown in colour, 20 cm long, have no visible tail, and have unmistakably large round ears. Come the first snowfall, pikas have a storehouse of dried veggies to help them through the long alpine winter (see p. 155).

Squirrels

The two most commonly seen animals in the Stein's forests are the northwestern chipmunk and the red squirrel. A chipmunk is easily identified by its striped head and back and upright tail when moving. Seeds, fruit, roots, and flowers are the primary food sources of this solitary ground-dwelling squirrel. Noticeably larger than the chipmunk (31 cm long vs 22 cm for the chipmunk), the vocal red squirrel actually has two coats, the summer one being a darker reddish-grey turning to a paler rusty grey in winter. Its food consists of conifer seeds supplemented by bark, fruits, buds, mushrooms, insects, bird eggs and baby rodents.

Unlike the diurnal northwestern chipmunk and red squirrel, the nocturnal northern flying squirrel is rarely seen. It is similar in size to the red squirrel and is a consumer of lichens, buds, fruits, mushrooms, and seeds. If located in flight, the flying squirrel is easily identified by its gliding motion as it extends its feet and uses the folds of skin attached from the front to rear feet for flight control.

Meadow vole
(*Microtus pennsylvanicus*)
A common resident of meadows, fields, and marshes. (N.W.P.S.)

Rodents

Mice and pack-rats

Rodents are probably the most numerous mammals, occuring in a variety of shapes, sizes, and forms. The Stein is inhabited by at least 11 rodents, the most common of which are the deer mouse, Cascade deer mouse, and bushy-tailed woodrat. Common in dry country from valley bottom to timberline, the reddish-brown coloured deer mice are nocturnal creatures perpetually seeking out tree buds and fruits, seeds, berries, centipedes, insects, and backpacker's granola. Deer mice are a primary food source for owls and weasels. High reproductive rates allow the deer mouse to sustain its populations. The much larger bushy-tailed wood rat (about 40 cm long, half of which is tail, whereas the deer mouse is only 20 cm long, including a 10 cm tail) is more assertive, brownish-grey in colour, and found primarily in coniferous forests. The foliage of deciduous and coniferous trees and shrubs, fruits, and seeds are this nocturnal rat's main food sources.

Also called "pack rat" because of its attraction to unusual objects, the wood rat can be a juggernaut of destruction as experienced by the author on several occasions. One night stands out: Camped at Avalanche Creek camp, I was awakened

Porcupine
(Erethizon dorsatum)
Fun to watch, but keep
children and Fido away
from those quills. (L.d.)

by a strange chewing noise outside. Soon it was apparent that a bushy-tailed woodrat was removing the shiny sliders on the tent fly lines, obviously fine additions to his collection. This was just the beginning, however. For reasons unknown to me, the rat proceeded to chew on the material of both the fly, which I soon retrieved into the tent for fear of it being entirely consumed, and then the tent itself! Despite strong language and numerous attempts to scare it off, the rat kept returning for more. The highlight of the evening for the rat, undoubtedly, was the tent's enraged occupant hiding by a rock at 4:00 a.m. in nothing more than his underwear, armed with a large stick. Fortunately, these rodents are constantly pursued by owls, weasels, and bobcats.

Voles and lemmings

Rarely seen but equally important to predator populations, voles and lemmings are mouse-like rodents found primarily in meadows, fields, and forests. Consumers of all varieties of vegetable matter, these primarily nocturnal mammals can be distinguished from other rodents by their short ears, smaller eyes, blunter heads, and shorter tails. Size depends on the species, but most voles and lemmings are approximately 15 cm long including a 4 cm long tail.

Porcupine

The unmistakable porcupine - readily identified by its long yellow and black quills - is the Stein's second largest rodent at a length of 75 cm, including a 20 cm tail. A resident of coniferous forests from valley bottom to the subalpine, porcupines eat leaves, twigs, green plants, and clover, resorting to chewing the bark off trees in the winter when their normal foliage food is gone. Contrary to popular belief, porcupines do not actually eat the bark. Rather, they strip it - often killing the tree in the process - so that they can eat the sweet cambium layer just beneath the bark.

Muskrat and beaver

Two aquatic rodents found in the Stein are the relatively small muskrat (length 55 cm, tail 25 cm) and the beaver, the largest rodent at a length of 105 cm, which includes a 45 cm tail. They are similar in build and colour, but are differentiated by their size and tail - the beaver's is large and flat while the muskrat's is narrow and long. Beaver and muskrat are found in slower moving streams and ponds. The area west of Stein

Lake is prime beaver habitat. Muskrat prefer aquatic vegetation and, when available, crayfish, frogs, and fish. Beavers, like porcupines, eat the cambium layer of deciduous trees as well as leaves and twigs. Both beaver and muskrat build homes given suitable conditions or else dig burrows in muddy banks. Muskrat and beaver are primarily nocturnal.

Marmot

The most commonly seen mammal in the Stein's alpine. The hoary marmot is an oversized, ground-dwelling squirrel. It is silvery grey with a black and white head and shoulders, has a bushy tail, and is about 70 cm long, 21 cm of which is tail. Marmots are often seen sunning themselves on boulders close to their underground dens. This close relative of the groundhog (woodchuck) fattens up for its long winter hibernation by eating grasses and almost any other green plant, especially towards the end of summer. Marmots are nicknamed "Whistler" because of their unmistakable shrill alarm whistle.

Weasels

Pound for pound (gram for gram?), weasels are the fiercest and most skilled predators. Eight species of these primarily nocturnal mammals are found in the Stein. In or near streams and lakeshore, look for mink (55 cm long, including a 18 cm tail) and river otter (110 cm long with a 42 cm tail) as they pursue small fish, muskrat, rodents, and amphibians. Distinguishing between these dark brown weasels is easy: The river otter is considerably larger. Both will venture into meadows in search of meadow voles.

Marten and skunk are found at lower elevations. The marten prefers forested areas, while the skunk normally stays in grassy and shrubby places. The reddish-brown marten, which often has a pale orange chest and light brown underside, consumes grouse, rodents, bugs, berries, and carrion. Marten are roughly 60 cm long and have an 18 cm long tail. The easily identified striped skunk (60 cm long, tail 23 cm) is more omnivorous in its diet, eating grasses, berries, leaves and buds, insects, rodents, fish, amphibians, bird eggs, and snakes.

Northwestern chipmunk
(*Tamias amoenus*)
Any visitor to the Stein is sure to see this common resident of the forest. (J.N.)

The solitary fisher, which despite its name rarely ever catches fish, is found primarily in the subalpine. Next to the wolverine, the chocolate brown or black coloured fisher is the second largest weasel at a length of almost one metre (35 cm tail). It pursues voles, deer mice and other small rodents, snowshoe hare, grouse, tree squirrels, and the occasional porcupine. Blueberries and grouseberries are other favourites when in season. Sharing the subalpine with the fisher is the short-tailed weasel, a much smaller (28 cm long, including an 8 cm tail) but equally skilled hunter of essentially the same diet. Unlike the fisher, which is active day and night, the short-tailed weasel hunts only at night. The most common of the weasels, the short-tailed weasel has a summer coat which is brown on top and white underneath, changing to all white for winter.

Throughout the watershed, the long-tailed weasel and the wolverine hunt smaller mammals. The primarily dark brown wolverine, while rarely seen, is sometimes mistaken for a small bear, but its disproportionately small head and bushy tail gives it away (see **The Opportunist on the Move**, p. 173). This opportunistic scavenger is about one metre long. Unmistakably "weasel like" with its 40 cm long body, longish tail (14 cm), and short legs and ears, the long-tailed weasel may occasionally be seen in meadows and on rock slopes. Its colour changes from a cinnamon brown top and white bottom in summer to an all white winter coat.

Dogs

Both the gray wolf and the coyote inhabit the Stein. These skilled hunters contrast in their adaptability. The coyote is increasing in number, while the wolf, like the grizzly, is becoming scarce since it too has lost most of its former range because of man's encroachment. Wolves are rarely seen (although sometimes heard), whereas coyotes may be seen from dawn to dusk, primarily in forested and grassy areas. The much maligned wolf hunts big game - deer and moose - but it also depends on a healthy population of hare, marmots, mice, and voles.

Coyotes, like wolves, hunt in groups, especially in winter. In summer, coyotes can be found in meadows pouncing on voles. Carrion and snowshoe hare are also consumed. The omnivorous coyote also ingests vegetable matter. Differentiate between these two by size. The wolf is 175 cm long and 1 metre tall at the shoulder. Coyotes are 120 cm and 60 cm respectively. Also compare tail shape: A coyote tail is proportionately longer, bushier, and is carried low, whereas the wolf's tail is carried straight. The coyote's fox-like look is distinguishable from the wolf's more square face.

Cats

Three wild felids are found in Canada: Cougar, lynx, and bobcat. The presence of these large solitary carnivores is indicative of the Stein's wilderness character. These shy, elusive cats prefer dense forest and brush, becoming active primarily from dusk to dawn. Both the lynx and bobcat are small compared to the cougar (the cougar is 230 cm long whereas bobcat and lynx are about 85 cm long). The cougar is also distinguished by its long (75 cm) tail; bobcat and lynx have short tails, no longer than 10 cm for the lynx and 20 cm for the bobcat.

Lynx and bobcat differ in colour. Bobcat are tawny and spotted in black while lynx are grizzled grey and buffy underneath. The healthy mule deer population of the Stein sustains the cougar. Snowshoe hare, porcupine, beaver, and, less frequently, moose supplement its diet (see **In Search of a Real Male**, p. 110, for more information on the cougar). Lynx and bobcat hunt smaller mammals. Snowshoe hare, grouse, duck, perching birds, and rodents are their main staples.

Moose
(*Alces alces*)
This relatively recent
arrival to southern B.C.
is unmistakable in both
size and appearance.
(N.W.P.S.)

Bears

Healthy populations of black and grizzly bear are found within the Stein. The black bear is smaller than the grizzly, its only natural predator. Apart from size, grizzlies can be distinguished by their patchy and streaky colouring. Colour variance is significant, from black to light brown, often with white tipped hairs. Black bears are sometimes cinnamon-brown. The grizzly, which resides primarily above timberline has a pronounced shoulder hump that black bears do not have and is larger (grizzlies are about 190 cm long and 130 cm at the shoulder whereas black bear are 170 cm and 95 cm respectively).

Black bears tend to be below treeline, presumably to avoid grizzly. Both bears are omnivores, with vegetable matter being the primary component of their diet. A grizzly's long claws allow it to easily dig roots and tubers, which it harvests regularly in the avalanche paths once the snow has left. Berries, whitebark pine seeds, fish, and the occasional mammal rounds out grizz's diet. A black bear depends more on sprouting plants, insects, and the buds or inner bark of shrubs and trees in spring and summer. In the fall, fruit, berries, and salmon are its main food sources.

Ungulates

Healthy populations of mule deer, mountain goat, and mountain sheep are found within the Stein. Moose are less abundant since they are normally restricted to their marsh and subalpine meadow habitat. Mule deer are the most commonly seen larger mammal throughout the valley bottoms. Only the bucks move to higher elevations for summer and early fall. Most easily identified by a large white rump patch and a black-tipped white tail, mule deer eat grasses and wildflowers in spring and summer and twigs and tree buds in winter.

The largest of the ungulate family at a length of 250 cm and shoulder height of 180 cm (we are talking big!), moose live in meadows and marshes, feeding on aquatic vegetation in summer and willows, aspen, and poplar in winter. Despite their size, moose are incredibly agile and quiet - you can travel through moose country and not see even one.

For much of the year mountain goat and sheep live at higher elevations. Distinguishing between the two is simple: Goats have long white coats while the more stocky sheep are light brown in summer and grey in winter. Also, goats sport black and pointed horns whereas male sheep have curved horns, often spiralling 360 degrees. They are similar in size, both standing about 100 cm at the shoulder and 175 cm in length. Grasses, wildflowers, and foliage are suitable for sheep; goats prefer grass and occasional subalpine fir needles and twigs.

PART IV:

BEFORE YOU GO

This section is mandatory reading!

BEFORE YOU GO

For your own safety and enjoyment and out of respect for the environment, a basic knowledge of backcountry travel skills, equipment, and ethics is essential. Take the time to read the following, especially the sections concerning ethics, and, if possible, the recommended readings.

PLANNING

Expectations

Prior to any backcountry trip, regardless of how long it is, each member of your group should have a clear picture of where he or she is going, how difficult and time consuming the trip will be, and what attractions and problems can be expected. Take the time to ensure everyone is informed. Most important is choosing a trip that the entire group is capable of. The limitations of the weakest member of your party should be your guide. Many of the accidents in the mountains result from people going beyond the ability and conditioning of one or more persons in the group. Know each member's limitations and plan accordingly.

Notice of plans

To plan correctly, obtain the necessary maps and read this guide at least once for its cautions and the trail and/or route information appropriate for your trip. Take note of the weather and season of travel information for your designated area. Leave a detailed description of your trip with a reliable person who will give the authorities the necessary information if you are not back by a specified time. Be sure to indicate when and where you expect to begin and finish the trip and account for bad weather delays in your return time, especially if going into the Stein's western alpine. Any last minute changes in plans should be left with the R.C.M.P. or Forest Service.

Group size and leadership

There is safety in numbers! While not as conducive to a wilderness experience and more damaging to the environment, a group of at least four is recommended when going for more than a day trip. Every member of your party should be familiar with basic back-country travel skills in map reading and compass work; take a course in backcountry navigation when in doubt. If the group has novices, it is a good idea to have a leader in order to make them feel comfortable.

PHYSICAL FITNESS

If you are not regularly active and shudder at the thought of putting a pack on your back, you had best not go any further than a day trip. Know your limits and stay within them. The Stein's diversity allows for easy trips, especially in the lower canyon, and masochistic bushwacks for those with such inclinations. Choose your trip, start slowly and increase the pace if you feel comfortable. Remember, this is not a competition.

ETHICS

Perhaps the greatest danger facing the Stein is not logging, but the potential abuse of the valley by the increasing numbers of individuals who do not practice minimal impact camping. While only a general guideline, the following should be your modus operandi in the backcountry. Also, educate yourself and others on the continually evolving code of ethics for wilderness travel. **The importance of this issue can not be overstated!!**

Pets

While Bowser may provide companionship and amusement, he is a disruptive force in the backcountry. Not only do dogs distract from other people's wilderness experiences, they also affect the wildlife. Fact: Ground-dwelling animals will often abandon their home if they detect a dog's scent. Plus, man's best friend is a well-known carrier of Giardiasis (see Water, below). Furthermore, your beloved pet could possibly endanger you and your party by aggravating a bear. In short, leave your dog at home.

Sanitation

The clear, unpolluted water of the Stein is one of its main attractions. Water purity is jeopardized, however, by people disposing their waste too close to rivers and streams. Giardia and other microbes are introduced into the water system by improperly disposing of wastes. In disposing of solid body waste there are three main concerns: Minimizing the chance of water pollution, minimizing the chance anything or anyone finding the waste, and maximizing the rate of decomposition. All means of disposal have their drawbacks. Since there are no toilet facilities in the Stein, be prepared to dig a hole approximately 10 - 15 centimetres deep and cover it with soil and other organic material. You should be at least 100 metres from any water source. **Very carefully** burn or pack out all toilet paper - it does not decompose as quickly as you may think. In the alpine, be sure to find as much organic soil as possible. Sanitary napkins should be wrapped in several layers of plastic and packed out.

Tread lightly

How and where you travel is important. Trails have been constructed, in part, to help limit erosion. Resist the temptation to walk around muddy sections or else you will break down the trail edge and widen the path. In the alpine, stay on the trail, if there is one. Otherwise, spread out so as to avoid stepping repeatedly on the same area, especially in the sensitive alpine meadows; alpine vegetation is particularly susceptible to erosion and takes a long time to recover. Avoid the temptation to cut the corners on the switchbacks of trails, so as to not further erosion. In general, look before you step.

The Stein has a wealth of historical cultural sites that should be treated with the same care as any museum. Especially sensitive are pictographs; do not touch the native people's lasting legacy. Similarly, respect private property both adjacent to and within the valley (you must cross private property when accessing the Stein from Lytton and Siwhe Creek).

Vegetation

Most appropriate to this topic is the old adage, "leave nothing but footprints, take nothing but pictures." In other words, leave everything as you found it. As is the case with all of man's destructive habits, it is not the act of one person that is damaging, but rather the cumulative effect of many doing the same thing.

Making camp

A clean, appropriately placed camp is an important part of minimal impact camping. Pitch your tent in designated areas or in places where you will not ruin the shrubs and trees. Resist the temptation to burn food scraps and garbage; often the scraps do not burn completely, resulting in garbage being left behind. Always keep your camp meticulously clean of food scraps so as to not attract unwanted visitors. The recent increase in mice and rat populations in the Stein is directly attributable to people's carelessness. Until you have had your pack chewed, your chocolate bars eaten, and your tent attacked, you have no idea what a problem these creatures can be. Don't be part of the problem!

Garbage

Perhaps the most distressing thing to see in the backcountry is the garbage of others. Be courteous, if you can pack it in, you can pack it out. Similarly, if you come across someone else's garbage, pack it out.

Fires

An integral part of the woods experience for many people is the beloved campfire. But the campfire is a destructive force. A curse on those who have needless fires in the backcountry. Never construct a fire in the fragile alpine environment - the small amount of organic material in this area cannot survive depletion by fire and the scar is permanent. For cooking, use a gas stove. If you do insist on a fire in the valley bottom, practice the following:

- Use already established sites or construct it close to a river, within the flood channel.

- Burn only wood from dead trees, being sure to collect the wood from a large area so as to minimize your impact.

- Keep it small. Bonfires are wasteful, dangerous, and certainly not romantic.

- Ensure that the fire is completely extinguished before leaving it.

- Smother it with lots of water. The fire hazard in the Stein is always high from June to October.

- Finally, think of the worsening greenhouse effect we are experiencing. Your fire may be small, but think of many fires ....

EQUIPMENT

Few people want to be a gear freak, but there are certain items that should be in your pack at all times. Proper equipment can make a real difference in comfort and safety. Seek out the advice of a reputable outdoor equipment store's staff if you have any questions - they are there to help you.

For any trip including day trips you should have the following:

•compass	•map	•sunblock	•first aid kit
•extra clothing	•sunglasses	•hat	•extra food
•water bottle	•moleskin	•knife	•fire starter
•waterproof matches	•flashlight or headlamp	•insect repellant •extra bulbs, batteries	•whistle

FOOTWEAR

Proper footwear and care can make or break your trip. If you are hiking the lower canyon for a day or overnight trip, lightweight hiking boots may be adequate. Trips involving a heavier pack and wetter, more difficult conditions require full-leather boots. Be sure to break in your footwear before going. Applying moleskin on sensitive spots, changing socks during the day, and keeping your feet dry and clean will help minimize blister formation. Two layers of socks are needed: The inner layer should be a thin, synthetic sock to keep your feet dry (cotton socks are not as desirable since they tend to abrade the skin when wet, but do aid in cooling the feet and therefore should be used in summer only), while the outer layer is usually a wool sock to absorb the abrading of the boot. Carry extra socks, even for day trips. Those venturing into the alpine should consider packing gaiters.

FOR OVERNIGHT TRIPS

1) Proper clothing. The layering principle, adding or removing layers of clothing depending on the weather and your activity level, is your guide in dressing properly for the outdoors. For the skin layer use synthetic (e.g., polyester or polypropylene) tops and bottoms if the weather is anything other than hot. Cotton can be justified for its cooling properties in hot weather, but beware of using it in wet and cold conditions because it offers no insulative value when wet, unlike synthetics and wool. The insulative or middle layer should consist of a synthetic fleece jacket or wool sweater, and the outer layer, which stops wind, rain, and snow, is best achieved with one of the "breathable" fabrics such as Entrant® or Gore-Tex®.

2) Sleeping bag and pad. Spend the money on a bag that will keep you warm in the places you are visiting. At least a -5 to -10 ° C temperature rating is needed if travelling in the alpine from June to September. For insulation between the ground and comfort for your aching bones and muscles use a close-celled foam pad or a lightweight inflatable air mattress.

3) A properly fitting pack. Internal frames are your best bet. External frames have their place on the flat and level, but are inappropriate for active use (try ski-touring with one).

4) Shelter. Modern technology has blessed us with many good tents. Those on a budget or going ultra light-weight may consider a tarp or bivy sack. If heading into the more bug-infested areas, you will definitely want no-see-um netting.

5) Cooking stove. Central to minimal impact camping is the use of a gas stove rather than a campfire for cooking. A dependable, field-maintainable single burner unit is all you need. Be sure to take extra fuel and spare parts, and learn how to maintain and fix your stove.

6) Odds and ends. Extra fuel, rope (at least 12 m), plenty of stuff sacks and plastic bags to pack your items in, and additional insulated clothing. Recommended but not essential are a small pack for daytrips, a repair kit - sewing materials, extra buckles, webbing, Freesole® (the fix everything wonder product), boot laces - and an emergency signal device such as flares.

BEAR COUNTRY TRAVEL

The Stein is home to a healthy population of grizzly and black bears. While they reside primarily within the remote parts of the watershed, they do wander down as far as the lower canyon in their perpetual quest for food. Fortunately, they are still wild - they fear you and want nothing to do with you. That changes, however, if the bear begins to associate humans with easily obtainable food. Read Stephen Herrero's *Bear Attacks: Their Causes and Avoidance*. At the very least you should :

- Leave the rifle at home. You should be practicing bear avoidance techniques, not crisis management. Herrero sums it up in saying, "Your best weapon to minimize the risk of bear attack is your brain."

- Make your presence known by making loud noise as you travel the trails and routes. Most bear attacks result from: 1) Suprising a bear and thereby aggravating it. 2) Disturbing a mother with cubs. 3) Interrupting a bear with food. You can reduce the chances of encountering a bear by letting it know you are in the area; if given the opportunity, bears will quickly vacate the scene. This is especially important in places where the bear cannot hear or smell you, such as noisy sections of river and dense vegetation.

- At camp: Cook at least 100 m downwind of your tent; suspend your food from trees at least 5 m above the ground and at least 100 m downwind from your tent (above treeline, seal all edible and fragrant items in several layers of plastic to minimize the smell and store well away from camp, ideally buried in a boulder field); leave your pack and cooking and eating clothes outside your tent; put all edible and fragrant items - including garbage, sunscreen, and soap - in your tree stash; pack out but don't burn your garbage - bears are attracted by even partially burnt foods; and don't camp where fresh bear signs (tracks, diggings, droppings) are present.

MEDICAL PROVISIONS AND INSECTS

A course in wilderness first aid is highly recommended. For longer trips, ensure that at least two people in your party are competent in first aid. Include in your first aid kit antihistamine to reduce swelling (wasps are found in several parts of the valley).

Ticks are a problem in the early season of May and June. These annoying little bugs are found primarily in grassy areas, where they wait for mammals to latch onto. Check your clothing regularly and if you find one embedded into your skin do not touch it with your hands - people have contracted diseases from ticks by handling them. Use tweezers (tissue or gauze otherwise) to grab the tick as close to the head as possible and pull it gently out. Do not twist while pulling. Ensure that all tick parts are removed from the wound and treat the affected area.

Hypothermia, the lowering of the body's core temperature, is of constant concern in the backcountry, especially in the alpine and in winter. Recognize the symptoms (slurred speech, stumbling, confused thinking, shivering, weakness, and shallow breathing) and assist the victim by removing wet clothes and providing warm shelter, keeping him or her warm - place the victim naked in a sleeping bag with another naked person in severe cases. Most important is to practice prevention by eating enough food, wearing warm and dry clothing, and covering your head, a major source of heat loss if uncovered.

Heat exhaustion may occur when an individual overheats (normally through physical exertion) or is exposed to a hot environment. This is a definite possibility in the eastern Stein. Dehydration (see Water and Nutrition below), inadequate salt intake, and lack of acclimatization make an individual more susceptible. Be sure to add salt to your food, carry salt tablets, and drink enough water. Taking a break during the mid-day and travelling in the morning and late afternoon is recommended.

WATER AND NUTRITION

One thing often overlooked by active people is maintaining sufficient fluid intake. Not only will your muscles benefit from proper water levels, but your energy level will also be higher. This is especially important on a hot summer day. As a general rule, adults should consume at least 4 litres of fluids per day.

Food: Complex carbohydrates are your key for optimum performance and easy packing, striving for a maximum calories per gram ratio (sorry, but espresso does not make the grade). Pasta, rice, cous cous, lentils, bulgar, oatmeal, granola... you get the idea. Take instant soup mixes and sauces for making the food somewhat palatable. Fruit leathers, chocolate, your grandmother's secret gorp mix, and breads and cheeses help break the monotony.

ROUTE FINDING & RIVER CROSSINGS

Several of the routes in this guide require solid route finding skills. Being able to correctly read the 1:50,000 maps and terrain is a skill that requires practice. Plus, in the event of limited visibility due to weather or dense vegetation, you should be able to use a compass to navigate to your destination. Take a course from the Federation of Mountain Clubs of B.C., read some of the books in the recommended reading section of this book, and go with people who have these skills.

Caution is required when crossing snow fields and glaciers. None of the summer routes and trails in this guide cross glaciers, but some will take you through snow fields. Your greatest concerns on the trails and routes are avalanches and cornices (overhangs of snow and ice that can give way without warning). Stay in the middle of broad ridges and look for signs of avalanche debris before passing under or across potentially dangerous slopes.

In crossing creeks look for a sturdy log and loosen your pack's straps, being ready to throw it off. If you do not feel comfortable, try it without the pack first. Try to land on the downstream side if you feel yourself falling. Walking or crawling forward is easier than moving sideways. Avoid crossing above logjams.

WATER

There have now been confirmed cases of Giardiasis ("Beaver Fever") in the Stein. This parasite, normally found on surface water, attaches to the inside of the small intestine and, less frequently, the gall bladder of most mammals. It enters water bodies through the feces of a carrier. Symptoms normally appear within approximately 15 days and include diarrhea, stomach cramps, lack of appetite, and weakness.

To avoid this nasty little critter always drink from the fastest part of the stream, reaching down several centimetres below the surface. You may also want to boil the water for five minutes or use a portable water filter (Katadyn® ceramic filters are your best bet; the new MSR Waterworks® filter may prove to be effective, but is a relatively unknown item at this time). Iodine and chlorine are less reliable due to pH and temperature differences. This is not to say that the Stein is stricken with bad water - the water is as pure as can be found anywhere. Giardiasis accompanies mammals, so it will be found in any wilderness. Humans contribute greatly to this problem by not properly disposing their personal waste (see Ethics above) and by bringing their dogs. In summary, the water is normally fine, but take the extra precautions when in doubt.

Recommended reading:

- Hampton, Bruce, and Cole, David. *Soft Paths*, Stackpole Books, 1988.
- Herrero, Stephen. *Bear Attacks: Their Causes and Avoidance*, Nick Lyons Books, 1985.
- Lachapelle, Edward R. *The ABC of Avalanche Safety*, The Mountaineers, 1969.
- Manning, Harvey. *Backpacking: One Step at a Time*, Vintage Books, 1980.
- Meyer, Kathleen. *How to Shit in the Woods*, Ten Speed Press, 1989.
- Wilkerson, James. *Medicine for Mountaineering*, The Mountaineers, 1975.

PART V:

RECREATIONAL INFORMATION

LOWER STEIN

Most people's first exposure to the Stein is via the lower canyon. The accommodating weather and terrain, easy access, and beautiful scenery make it the obvious destination for a day or weekend of relaxing exploration.

Ecological overview: The lower Stein, from the mouth to just west of Stryen Creek's confluence with the Stein and including Van Winkle Flat, is part of the driest and hottest ecological zone of B.C., the bunchgrass biogeoclimatic zone. Grassland predominates with bluebunch wheatgrass being the dominant bunchgrass on undisturbed sites. Sage-brush is also common, but is more prevalent on overgrazed areas. Ponderosa pine and Douglas fir are the only trees able to grow in this dry climate.

1. Stein Bridge to Confluence of the Stein and Fraser

Many trails can be found in the area around the Stein Bridge, 5.6 km north of the ferry on the West Side Road. The following two descriptions take you to the mouth of the Stein.

These trails cross Indian reserve property and should be treated with the same respect as any private property deserves. Year-round hiking is possible on these trails, which are suitable for all ages. Time: Each trip, 45 minutes to 1 hour round-trip.

Stein - Fraser Confluence (A.B.)

Winter Villages

The mouth of the Stein has a rich history, for it was on these banks that the Nlaka'pamux lived for millenia. Based out of pithouses - large houses built deep into the ground and often supplemented by cooking facilities, storage areas, and hearths - the native people lived here primarily during the winter months, spending much of the rest of the year hunting and gathering in the mountains. The houses varied in size, with most accommodating 15 to 30 persons. Some exceptionally large houses held 60 to 80 people. Apparently, the north bank of the Stein was an ideal winter village site given the close proximity to fishing, hunting, gathering, and abundance of water, fuel, and construction materials. Plus, winter winds were less prevalent here and the soil drained well. To date, approximately 70 pit house remnants, large circular depressions in the ground, have been recorded by the B.C. Heritage Conservation Branch.

From South Side of Bridge:

Next to the bridge's south end is a parking area and adjacent campsite. The easiest approach to gain access to the mouth is to proceed south from the bridge for 0.2 km (0.1 mi.), where a rough road intersects the West Side Road.

This road drops and winds down to the rivers in only 0.6 km (0.4 mi.), offering no problems to travellers on foot or in two-wheel drive vehicles. Here you will find a well-used campsite and easy access to fishing.

Confluence and 1986 Stein Festival Site

From the north side of the bridge proceed towards a brick pumphouse building next to the road. A trail on the bank behind the building should be visible. Hop the fence and climb the small slope via the trail for an elevation gain of about 25 m (75 ft). Proceed downstream, crossing the bench you are on for 60 m (200 ft), at which point you will find a road. Follow the road down to a large flat, open bench just above the banks of the Stein. The prayer circle here was part of the 1986 Stein Festival. Numerous camping sites are found in the immediate area.

2. North Shore Trail

Attractions: Accessibility; good views of lower canyon.
Cautions: Steep in places - exercise caution if taking children.
Access: From first bend in West Side Road 0.5 km (0.3 mi.)
north of Stein Bridge. **Season**: Year round. **Rating**: Easy -
moderate. **Distance and time**: 2.3 km (1.4 mi.); 1 hour - 1 hour
30 minutes one way. **Elevation gain**: 30 m (100 ft); 75 m (250
ft) on return. **Map**: 92 I/5.

Finding the beginning of this trail requires following the
West Side Road from the north side of Stein Bridge to the first
sharp bend in the road 0.5 km (0.3 mi.) north of the bridge.
Take the rough road that intersects the West Side Road at this
point and follow it uphill through a pine forest and underneath
the hydro power lines.

Be sure to take the right fork in the road, 0.2 km (0.1 mi.)
below the power line. Continue straight uphill, looking for
orange markers on the trees. This is the beginning of the trail.
The West Side Road should be visible from here. At approximately 0.5 km (0.3 mi.) avoid a path on your left that descends
to the river. The trail ascends before levelling off 0.6 km (0.4
mi.) from the trailhead. You then start descending gently as the
trail curves around the side of the hill and moves parallel to the
river below. The open Ponderosa pine forest allows for views
of the main trail, Van Winkle Flat, and sharp bends of the Stein.
You are now approximately 0.8 km (0.5 mi.) from the start and
1.5 km (0.9 mi.) from the terminus of the trail.

Alligator lizard
(*Elgaria coerulea*)
Slender and long (up
to 10 cm) in body,
it is found in open rock
areas, especially near
forest. Snacks on in-
sects and spiders. Like
the western skink, the
alligator lizard can shed
its tail, apparently in an
attempt to distract a
predator. (R.B.C.M.)

Approximately 0.4 km (0.3 mi.) of descent takes you past
rock outcrops about 75 m (250 ft) above the river. A couple of
minutes past the outcrops is a junction in the trail at a large
Ponderosa pine. To continue to the trail's terminus next to the
river, take the left fork which descends for 0.8 km (0.5 mi.) to
the flat bench next to the river. Several campsites are found
here. The junction's right fork is a well-beaten game trail that
climbs to several viewpoints above (see Bluff Trail description
that follows).

3. Bluff Trail

At the junction by the large Ponderosa pine 1.5 km (0.9 mi.)
from the trailhead and 0.8 km (0.5 mi.) from the trail's
terminus, proceed uphill along the right fork. Go left at the first
junction 0.2 km (0.1 mi.) from the start. A well-defined game

Stryen Creek Bridge (N.B.)

trail leads to atop a prominent ridge, 1.0 km (0.6 mi.) from the start. Avoid an old trail on your left as you continue uphill for another 0.1 km to the top of the bluff. Fine views of the lower canyon, Van Winkle Flat, and the greater Lytton area are gained from here. Those wanting to explore further can ascend the trail-less ridge, keeping in mind that there is no water in this area.

4. Stryen/Stein Divide Ridge

Attractions: Excellent views of Lytton and surrounding area. **Cautions**: Loose footing; some route finding necessary; carry water. **Access**: From rock outcrop 30 m west of Stryen Bridge (see Trailhead to Cable Crossing description, trip # 8). **Season**: April to October. **Rating:** Moderate. **Distance and time**: Approximately 1.3 km (0.8 mi.); 1 hour 15 minutes - 2 hours. **Elevation gain**: 600 m (2000 ft). **Map**: 92 I/5.

This steep climb to the two small summits on the ridge between the Stein River and Stryen Creek offers excellent views of the lower canyon, the Thompson and Fraser rivers, Lytton, Botanie Mountain, and Stryen Creek.

Approximately 30 m west of the Stryen Creek Bridge is a rock outcrop. Locate a trail just to the east of the rock and begin ascending the lower reaches of the ridge. At first, the ridge is not entirely obvious due to the forest cover. Soon the terrain temporarily flattens and the vegetation opens up. Continue ascending in a southwest direction up the broad ridge line. At 600 m (2000 ft) the ridge narrows. Exercise caution past here; those unsure of their footing should not proceed further.

Atop the first summit, elevation 780 m (2600 ft), the second summit is close at hand to the southwest. Descend 15 m (50 ft) into the gully between the summits and ascend the 25 m (80 ft) needed to gain the second summit. Return to the Stein via the same route used to ascend - the northern slopes are loose and bushy. And on your way down consider the problems of the road builder given the task of constructing a road over the ridge, as proposed by the Forest Service.

5. Trailhead to "The Forks," Stryen Creek

Attractions: Enjoyable hiking in pine and fir forests of lower sections of trail; the enchanting forest of The Forks; interesting geology. **Cautions:** Active slide area with steep slopes below "The Forks;" bear country; carry water. **Access:** From Stein Trailhead parking lot. **Season:** Late May - October. **Rating:** Easy - moderate. **Distance and time:** About 6.5 km (4.1 mi.), 1 hour 30 minutes - 2 hours 30 minutes. **Elevation gain:** 640 m (2100 ft). **Maps:** 92 I/5 and 92 I/4.

Douglas fir
(Pseudotsuga menziesii)
The most commonly seen tree in B.C. Identification: Symmetrical young trees up to 15 cm in diameter have smooth, grey/brown bark and resin blisters. Older trees have thick (up to 30 cm!) deeply fissured, reddish/brown bark, and heavy limbs. Native people used Douglas fir pitch for torches, branches for harpoon shafts and saplings for dipnets; green saplings are flexible enough to be moulded in to a circular shape. (N.B.)

For those wanting to get off the more frequented main Stein trail and explore a lesser known and yet still acccessible area, this may be the answer.

This hike initially crosses reserve property before connecting with a well-constructed old mining trail. **Please respect this private property and be very careful near the water channels since they carry the drinking water for many local people.** From the parking lot at the main Trailhead proceed east on the Stein Trailhead access road for 0.3 km (0.2 mi.) (towards the hydro power lines). Turn south on to the road from the south and ascend to the bench. Follow the road south as it crosses under the power line and then moves parallel to it. Avoid a rough road to the east, pass under the power line again, and cross a small water channel. Just past the water channel and 0.5 km (0.3 mi.) from the beginning of the bench is a rough road

The cabin at the Stryen Creek Forks (D.T.)

on your right - turn here and move in a westerly direction towards the more vegetated areas and away from the power line. 100 m past the last turnoff the road crosses a water channel, turns and moves alongside the channel. Eventually you begin a gentle ascent while moving roughly parallel to the water channel.

An open forest soon greets you as you continue moving west towards Stryen Creek. At the point the road becomes less discernable, follow it into the forest, **but avoid going down the bank into the Stryen Creek gully directly west**. Go left into the trees, cross the water channel, and move in a west-south-west direction towards another water channel only 80 m distant. Move west along its north side for 30 m to a rough crossing above a small body of water. Now move downstream to a road 30 m distant and follow it to where it intersects another road and an unlocked gate, elevation 345 m (1140 ft.). The worst route finding is now behind you.

Proceed up the road which briefly levels off and then brings you to a junction; go left and continue climbing to another junction 0.2 km (0.1 mi.) past the previous junction. Proceed along the right hand road, across an easy grade in open forest. 0.5 km (0.3 mi.) further and 1.5 km (0.9 mi.) from the gate, the road narrows to a trail.

The trail then crosses a rocky area, moves around blowdown, levels off briefly, and crosses more rock in the next 1.2 km (0.8 mi.). Soon you come to an open area with a talus slope ahead. Ascend over rocky terrain, including an open slide. The large talus slopes near this area are a good example of cliff face erosion; the talus slopes are the fractured remains of a rock

Bracket Fungi
Throughout any forest one is sure to see these semicircular growths on older trees and logs. Actually, these structures are fruiting bodies produced by mold colonies that extend for kilometres within the tree. Rarely recognized for their valuable role in the cycle of the forest, fungi such as bracket fungi are continually changing the landscape by breaking down the trees' cell walls. Ultimately, the tree falls, decomposes into soil, and provides the base for future generations of vegetation. (G.F.)

slide from cliff faces above. You are now 3.9 km (2.4 mi.) from the gate and 0.7 km (0.4 mi.) from "The Forks." Now the terrain becomes more demanding as the trail crosses a boulder field and ascends more steeply. Two switchbacks, elevation 920 m (3050 ft), immediately past the boulderfield are followed by an ascent up steep slopes that are dangerously active. Exercise caution through this section. The trail here is vague in places - some flagging tape identifies the correct route, but it is not consistently marked. A third switchback brings you close to the rise at the top of the slopes, 0.6 km (0.4 mi.) from the boulderfield below the slopes. A gradual descent from the rise to "The Forks" junction is easily completed in a few minutes. You are now 6.5 km (4.1 mi.) from the Trailhead parking lot. Several camping sites are close at hand in this beautiful cedar grove forest. See the West Fork description for accessing the cabin, which was constructed in 1932 by Jimmy Johnson and served as a teamsters' stopover for the Lytton Gold Mine.

6. Stryen Creek, East Fork

Attractions: Alpine meadows; good views. **Cautions**: Wet terrain; variable weather; bear country. **Access**: From "The Forks" (see trip # 5 for access). **Season**: Late June to September. **Rating**: Moderate. **Distance and time**: To meadows before mining camp, 6.0 km (3.8 mi.), 3 - 4 hours; to lakes, approximately 7.5 km (4.8 mi.), 4 - 5 hours. **Elevation gain**: To meadows, 570 m (1900 ft); to lakes, 720 m (2400 ft). **Map**: 92 I/4.

While quite limited in views for the first 2.9 km (1.8 mi.), the East Fork trail of Stryen Creek offers numerous opportunities for alpine exploration. The trail is, for the most part, easily followed until it disappears in the meadowed slopes below Mt. Roach.

The beginning of the trail was not obvious in the summer of 1990. From "The Forks" backtrack to the Stryen Creek trail. From here a boulder-strewn slope on your left should be visible. The trail starts on the hillside, but may be obstructed by windfall and boulders. Once past this part the trail is clearly identifiable.

The trail climbs at a gradual pace until 1.2 km (0.8 mi.) from the start and then increases in steepness. Another 0.3 km (0.2 mi.) brings you to a point above the cascading falls of Stryen Creek's east channel. The trail switchbacks before straightening out, soon offering fine views of Mt. Roach's northeast face.

2.4 km (1.5 mi.) from the start is a collapsed bridge across the creek. The bridge offers safe crossing in low-water, but exercise caution in spring - it may be impassable at this point.

Having crossed the creek you are now going to follow along its west side. Your destination, the valley east of Mt. Roach, should be apparent now as the east slopes of Mt. Roach and the west slopes of the peak southeast of Mt. Roach form the boundaries of the East Fork. Some views are gained as the trail stays within 100 - 150 metres of the creek. The trail becomes less obvious and overgrown by the time you reach the corduroy (dilapidated wooden walkway) 0.6 km (0.4 mi.) past the bridge. The footing is wet through here - proper footwear is a requisite. Just past the corduroy is a small boulder field. Stay close to the creek through here.

More trees and less identifiable sections of trail make for slower going for the remainder of the distance to the mining camp, 6.0 km (3.8 mi.) from the start. Camping can be found in the meadows 0.4 km (0.3 mi.) before the mine camp remnants and just after the mine camp. The lakes at the end of the valley are another 1 - 2 hours hike. Time permitting, advance to these lakes, which offer more accommodating camping and beautiful views of Mt. Nikaia.

6. Stryen Creek, West Fork

Attractions: Access to Stein's south divide and Skihist and Pelushkwohap Mountains. **Cautions**: Bushy and rocky trail; bear country. **Access**: From "The Forks" (terminus of trip #5). **Season**: Late June to September. **Rating**: Moderate - difficult. **Distance and time**: To rockslide at 1385 m (4550 ft), 3.0 km (2.3 mi.), 1 hour 30 minutes - 2 hours; to cabin approximately 4.5 km (2.3 mi.), 3 - 4 hours. **Elevation gain**: To rock slide, 410 m (1370 ft.); to cabin about 510 m (1700 ft). **Map**: 92 I/4.

A rough trail still exists on this fork of Stryen Creek and can be followed with some difficulty to the cabin remains 4.5 km (2.3 mi.) distant. At "The Forks" junction move towards the bank of Stryen Creek and proceed upstream 60 m before crossing the creek on a large log. 100 m past the crossing turn left and move uphill past the cabin, soon reaching a rock field. The trail then switchbacks 3 times, passes a small section of blowdown, and switchbacks again more steeply in the next 0.6 km (0.4 mi.). Continue ascending over rock slides until the trail levels off briefly as you pass by a side-valley 1.8 km (1.2 mi.) from the start.

Horse fly
(Hybomitra spp)
Few insects are as aggravating as the horsefly, which will sometimes follow you for hours across the subalpine and alpine in hope of getting a bite. They are big (up to 2 cm long) and tough - this one can withstand a severe stomping and come up flying. (M.M.)

Exercise caution as you cross the next rock slide and then descend into a brushy area, elevation 1370 m (4500 ft). The remaining 0.6 km (0.4 mi.) of measured trail takes you past cabin ruins, and beside the creek, which you must follow to the rock slide at 1385 m (4550 ft). At this point, the valley begins to open up and can be explored much further, especially by those seeking the alpine further south.

> *"Devoted though we must be to the conservation cause, I do not believe that any of us should give it all our effort or heart... Let us save at least half of our lives for the enjoyment of this wonderful world which still exists. Leave your dens, abandon your cars and walk out into the mountains, the deserts, the forests, the seashores. Those treasures still belong to all of us. Enjoy them to the full, stretch your legs, enliven your hearts - and we will outlive the greedy swine who want to destroy it all in the name of what they call growth."*
>
> *Edward Abbey*

West fork of Stryen Creek (L.K.)

STEIN RIVER LOWER CANYON

Contour Interval: 500 feet (150 meters)

Scale 1:75 000   1 cm = 750 metres

0   .5   1 mile   2   3
0   1 km   2   3   4   5   6

Legend:
- ↟ Cabin
- ▲ Campsite
- ⌁ Trail; Switchback
- --- Route
- ⌢ Creek; Stream
- ▬ River
- ● Lake
- vp Viewpoint

FERRY SCHEDULE

Daily 06:00 -> 22:15

Meal Breaks

9:30 ->10:00
17:00 -> 17:30

Map labels:

LYTTON

FERRY

Hwy. #12

Fraser River

Thompson River

Trans-Canada Hwy.

↓ Hope

↑ Lillooet

Botanie Valley ↑

N MN

21°

Confluence

Stein Bridge

Indian Reserve

PARKING & TRAILHEAD

West Side Road

BC Hydro Powerline

Van Winkle Flats

1500 ft (450 m)

Nohomin Creek

Stryen Creek

Seasonal

"Devils Staircase"

5000 ft (1500 m)

1500 ft (450 m)

1500 ft (450 m)

900 ft (900 m)

"Christina Falls"

Boulder Field

Steep

"The Forks"

East Fork

Cord Wood

Bridge Collapsed

West Fork

5000 ft (1500 m)

Mt. Roach 8672 ft (2600 m)

Stein River

Teaspoon Creek

6000 ft (1800 m)

Akasik Mtn. 8100 ft (2430 m)

Earl's Cabin

Earl Creek

200 ft (600 m)

Cable Crossing

Klein's Cabin

① ② ③ ④ ⑤ ⑥ ⑦ ⑧ ⑨

TRAILHEAD TO STEIN LAKE

The trail system extending from Stein Trailhead to Stein Lake provides access to the accommodating and culturally rich lower canyon, diverse mid-valley forests, and scenic Stein Lake area. Trips in this area vary from simple half-day hikes in the lower canyon to 10 day ventures into the further reaches of the valley. Please tread lightly through this area - it sees the vast majority of use in the Stein, and it is already showing sign of backpackers not practicing minimal impact camping.

Ecological overview: Extending from the banks of the Fraser River into the middle of the Stein, the Interior Douglas fir zone is the most predominant zone encountered along the Stein Trailhead to Stein Lake trail system. This zone is characterized by widely spaced Douglas fir and Ponderosa pine trees. Cedar groves and stands of northern black cottonwood become more common as one travels west. The much wetter Coastal Western Hemlock zone, which extends from west of Nesbitt Creek to Stein Lake has a more dense forest canopy and ground cover. Mixed stands of hemlock, spruce, cedar, and fir predominate in this zone.

8. Trailhead to Cable Crossing

Attractions: Easy access; spectacular rapids and chutes; steep canyon walls; easy hiking for even non-hikers; reliable weather; numerous camping sites; nonstop river watching. **Cautions:** Hot summer weather (hat and sunscreen are essential); loose footing on talus crossings; carry water since the river is not always accessible. **Access:** From Trailhead, near Lytton. **Season:** March to November. **Rating:** Easy to moderate. **Distance and time:** To west of "Devil's Staircase," 5.3 km (3.3 mi); 2 hours - 3 hours 30 minutes; to Earl Creek, 10.8 km (6.8 mi); 3 hours 30 minutes - 5 hours; to cable crossing, 13.2 km (8.3 mi); 4 - 6 hours. **Elevation gain:** 355 m (1200 ft). **Map:** 92 I/5.

Stein Trailhead (A.B.)

Starting at the Trailhead, elevation 230 m (750 ft), on the south side of the Stein, you are surrounded by the Ponderosa pine, bunchgrass, sage, and Saskatoon berry of the Interior's dry benchlands. This basically flat trail allows even the non-hiker to appreciate the beauty of the valley. Camping spots are as close as 10 minutes from the Trailhead.

Descending along a clear path towards the river, the roar of the turbulent water grows as you pass through the Ponderosa pine and Douglas fir above the river. Approximately 100 m (330 ft) along, the trail from Earlscourt Farm is on your left. Avoid the remains of an old bridge crossing Stryen Creek, 0.3 km (0.2 mi) from the trailhead, turning left away from the river to the new bridge. Known locally as Last Chance Creek, or **naikzakxn** to the Nlaka'pamux, meaning "to fall a log across," Stryen Creek originates in the alpine south of the Stein's lower canyon. Immediately past the bridge is a large rock outcrop. According to Harlan Smith, an archaeologist who worked in the Stein area in 1897, native boys and girls came here to wash with fir boughs during their puberty rituals. This site is also the first pictograph panel found on this trail.

Saskatoon berry
(Amelanchier alnifolia)
Commonly found in dry openings where it grows in clusters to heights of 2 - 3 m. Easily identified in April and May when white blossoms cover the bush. By July, berries are a dull red turning to a ripe black in early August. In the absence of flowers and berries, look for the Saskatoon's leaves, which are notched on top. Native people used the Saskatoon's wood for lining steam pits and protecting spears and arrows.(R.H.)

At 1.5 km (0.9 mi) a smooth flat rock outcrop brings you next to the river. Take time to feel the power of the river here. The next 2.3 km (1.4 mi) take you along the flat benches of the old river bed, which were formed when the river was much larger and more powerful than it is now. At this point, 3.9 km (2.4 mi) from the Trailhead, the ascent of the "Devil's Staircase" (or "Big Slide" to the native people) section of the trail begins. A trail to the right leads to a large camping area close to the river. To continue, go left and begin ascending. Be sure to carry water; for at least 30 minutes there will be none.

Having climbed via two switchbacks to approximately 400 m (1300 ft), you now encounter a large talus field. Careful with your footing here, especially in wet weather (children may require extra assistance through this section). From the top of the talus slope descend into a rock gully and pass through trees into the wet area of "Christina Creek," 0.6 km (0.4 mi) past the top of the talus slope. The trail continues above the river for 0.3 km (0.2 mi), taking you over another talus slope and above steep slopes that drop precipitously to the river below. The descent should be taken carefully - the footing is loose. A fallen log is on your right near the bottom of the descent and an island in the river is visible.

Wolf lichen
(Letharia vulpina)
This very colourful resi-
dent is undoubtedly the
most visible lichen in the
Stein. (A.D.)

To experience what is undoubtedly a "power spot" by any definition, cross the fallen log and proceed downstream approximately 100 m. Here, at the base of two cliffs, are two large pictograph panels. This location is known as **ts'ets'ekw'** which translates into "markings." **Please show respect for these priceless native artifacts by not touching or marking them. The importance of this matter cannot be overstated!** See **Pictographs of the Stein**, p. 32 for more information on the rock paintings.

Returning to the main trail description, the trail now returns to the river. Just 0.5 km (0.3 mi) past the bottom of the "Devil's Staircase" is a great view of the river coming into a tight turn. After passing through a cedar grove, you will come to a flood channel. Cross a small seasonal creek and resume a parallel direction to the river. A pond is visible on your right as you enter the forest again. Large boulders and logs near a small island are on your right as you once more move next to the Stein. Proceed to cross a small creek and ascend over a boulder field before reaching the teepee campsite, 8.3 km (5.1 mi) from the Trailhead. A food rope, fire circle, numerous tent sites, easy access to the river, and beautiful views are found at this popular site. In early spring, a waterfall descends lightly from the steep canyon walls on the north side of the river opposite the teepee.

Granitic rock's great strength and the wide spacing of joints within it results in very large blocks and boulders - as shown in this view of the lower Stein River (D.T.)

Lions in the Stein?

If you're prone to hiking with your head down while travelling the lower Stein trail during the warm months, you will probably have noticed tiny, conical pits along the trail. These distinctive structures occur wherever there is exposed dry, sandy, and loose soil. They range in diameter from one to six cm and are often found clustered together. What you may not have realized is that at the bottom of each of these pits is a tiny insect, waiting to seize and consume any other insect unfortunate enough to fall in. Each pit is basically a food funnel whose architect is the larva (juvenile) of an ant lion (family Myrmeleontidae, order Neuroptera). Ant lions are wary, and quick to disappear from their pit when disturbed. However, if you were able to catch one, you would see a small (1 - 7 mm long) sack with relatively large hollow jaws, through which prey juices are sucked. Tiny legs propel the ant lion backwards, resulting in a "rowing" action through the soil. If a small insect (e.g. an ant) falls into the pit, it will probably slide to the bottom and be seized immediately by the ant lion. Or it will attempt to run up the steep sides of the pit, but the walls will crumble and carry it back towards the waiting ant lion. Indeed, the ant lion deliberately encourages these "mini-landslides" by flicking sand particles onto the pit wall ahead of its struggling prey. Ant lions use smaller, more landslide-prone particles for lining their pit walls, and throw the slightly larger sand particles outside of the pit. If you carefully inspect the pit's periphery, you can probably see the larger, ejected sand grains, as well as the shrivelled corpses of the ant lion's recent meals. The size of the pit is a good indication of the ant lion's present size. Ant lion larvae are remarkably resistant to starvation and can survive for weeks without food. Once the ant lion larva has grown big enough, it pupates in the soil, and transforms into a winged adult resembling a damselfly. Adults mate and lay their eggs in the soil, where larvae hatch out to begin life "in the pits." So, think about these tiny, innovative architects dotting the trail along the lower Stein, and tread lightly.

Ralph Cartar

To continue past the teepee site, cross the flat, dry benchlands for 0.9 km (0.6 mi) before ascending a small hill. The trail levels off, allowing views of the river below. Teaspoon Creek lies 0.3 km (0.2 mi) beyond the hill. A cathedral-like grove of cedar trees and numerous camping spots make this a popular and enjoyable rest area. The trail is not clear through this grove, however.

Earl's cabin
The original Earl's cabin was built by Fred Earl, a trapper and prospector, probably related to the Earl family of Earlscourt Farm. He died while in service overseas in World War I. Fred reportedly took $12,000 in gold from Earl Creek and left a gold cache, which has not been found despite numerous attempts. Today, the outlines of two other structures and a recent reconstruction of the original cabin are all that remain. (A.B.)

You will then move away from the Stein to cross the creek again over another small bridge with a large boulder on the south side. Move beside a side channel and cross two more channels before resuming a parallel route to the river. A small island should be on your right as you come close to the river again. 1.2 km (0.8 mi) past Teaspoon Creek is Earl's Cabin, which has several suitable camping sites. The clearing here offers opportunities for wildlife observation. You are now 10.7 km (6.7 mi) from the Trailhead.

A few minutes of easy hiking brings you to Earl Creek. Follow the trail up the south bank to a bridge with a railing. Constructed by the Forest Service in 1978, this bridge can be slippery when wet; caution is required, especially if you are part of a group with children. The trail then follows the bank on the north side for 30 m before moving back towards the flats. A clear and flat trail for the next 1.3 km rewards those coming this far.

At this point the trail comes close to the river where rock bluffs extend to the river's edge. This is a magical spot. The pictographs on the rock walls are made even more impressive by the nearby rapids. From here the cable crossing is only 15 minutes away. Caution is needed in crossing a small boulder field immediately after the rock bluffs. At the crossing campsite, elevation 585 m (1950 ft), you will find a foodloft, fire circle, and several campsites. Klein's cabin is situated on an island 200 - 300 m west of the main site.

Making Use of All the Parts

As on the coast, the fibrous bark of western red-cedar was an important material [to the Nlaka'pamux]. It was stripped off the trees in large sheets. The thick outer bark was used as roofing for pithouses, and to line earthen pit-house walls. It was also used as temporary flooring, for sitting and kneeling on in canoes, and piled up, as bedding. Crude vessels were made of it for bailing out canoes. The inner bark was shredded and used for making "slow matches." Cedar fibre, and large, flat sheets of pounded cedar bark were found at Thompson burial sites. Sometimes ponchos, cloaks, bodices, and aprons were made from cedar inner bark, which was rubbed, beaten to soften it, then split into strips of desired width.

Turner, Nancy, et al, *Thompson Ethnobotany*, Royal B.C. Museum, 1990, p.96.

Klein's Cabin

One of the early trappers from whom we have learned of the Stein is Adam Klein. His landmark cabin, which he constructed in 1953 with the help of his son, reminds us of earlier times. Klein first trapped in the Stein in 1925 at only 18 years of age, having left his home in southern Saskatchewan after an argument with his brother and father. After learning the ways of the woods under Young Easter Hicks, a veteran trapper of the Stein, Klein worked his own traplines for the next 12 years. Klein's two main lines took him west from Stein Lake to Tundra Lake and south into the Rutledge Creek Valley, trapping marten, muskrat, and beaver.

9. Cable Crossing to Ponderosa Shelter

Attractions: The ecologically rich mid-valley forests; views of valley & canyon walls. **Cautions**: Loose rock on boulder-field crossings; parts are frequently flooded in spring. **Access**: North side of cable crossing, 4 - 6 hours (13.2 km) from the Trailhead. **Season**: Best April - October. **Rating**: Easy to moderate. **Distance and time**: 7.8 km (4.9 mi); 2 - 4 hours. **Elevation gain:** About 60 m (200 ft). **Map**: 92 I/5.

The Cable Crossing

Upgraded in 1986, as part of the trail work of the Western Canada Wilderness Committee, under the direction of Ken Lay, and the Lytton Indian Band, the cable crossing is a landmark of the Stein. While a huge improvement over the earlier crossing that existed from 1968 to 1986, caution is required.

Be sure to assist children and weaker members of your party when using the crossing. The car is intended for a single adult with a pack. Grab only the haul rope and keep hands away from the steel cable. When finished, ensure that the car is returned to the middle and not left secured at one end.

Ponderosa pine
(Pinus ponderosa)
There is no mistaking the "jigsaw puzzle" bark of the Ponderosa pine. (R.S.)

The lower cable crossing (G.F.)

As you move past the cable crossing and leave the lower canyon, the Stein changes character. The slow, meandering river of the mid-Stein replaces the turbulent waters of the lower valley. Note the difference between the water-eroded, V-shaped lower canyon and the glacier-eroded, U-shaped mid-valley as you head west.

The trail starts immediately above the platform of the cable crossing, on the north side. For several minutes move along the side of a hill, passing large Douglas fir. Rough camping sites without food ropes are found further along near the high water channels. Klein's Cabin is soon visible on the far bank.

A large S bend in the river occurs just past the cabin, 0.4 km (0.3 mi) west of the cable crossing. Called **stl'imin** (approximate pronunciation is "klemmen") - meaning to "ford the river" - this was the site of the first Stein bridge. Built by Urban Hicks, Walter Issac, and Jimmie Johnson in 1942 to give access to the Silver Queen Mine, the bridge was washed out in 1948. A second bridge was built downstream at the site of the present cable crossing after World War II. It too suffered a similar fate in 1968. Next, you will pass a boulder field before moving onto the flat next to the river; the surroundings become wetter through this area. The trail continues to be clearly defined as you move along the river bank. Excellent views of steep cliff faces on the opposite side are found here.

Gently rolling, forested benches with several creeks make up the terrain for the next 20 - 30 minutes. Fickle Creek and West Fickle Creek are first crossed. These creeks are not dependable water sources. Only 0.7 km (0.4 mi) past West Fickle Creek is Shelter Creek, a reliable source. A small bridge crosses here. As you continue through open forest, the trail comes close to both the river and rock bluffs that extend to the river's edge. Abundant horse tail is evident as you move alongside the slow tranquil river. Look for signs of beaver activity here. A large poplar with beaver gnawings is located approximately 15 minutes west of Shelter Creek. About 2.0 km west of Shelter Creek is Waterfall Creek and a crude campsite with an emergency shelter under a large boulder, a fire circle, and a food rope. There are few suitable tent sites here.

Camping on the river banks of the mid-valley (F.S.)

In spring this area can be wet as you cross the several channels of the creek. 10 - 15 minutes, 0.4 km (0.3 mi), more hiking takes you next to a beaver pond. A large scar on the south side of the valley should be visible from here. Continuing westward, move towards the rock slopes and begin the ascent to "Snake Bluffs," approximately 20 m (70 ft) above the flood plains. These bluffs give great views of the valley bottom. Continue along the bluffs by sidehilling and then carefully descending to the valley bottom. You are now 5.3 km (3.3 mi) from the cable crossing and 2.5 km (1.6 mi) from Ponderosa Shelter. The trail then proceeds towards the river, crossing the floodplains and continuing alongside the river.

For 0.5 km (0.3 mi) move next to the river bank on a flat, well-defined trail. A second small ascent is needed, taking you 15 - 20 m above the floodplains. From this vantage point you can see the clusters of black cottonwood that predominate the mid-valley floor. Aspen, birch, Douglas fir, and western red cedar are also found in this wet area. After descending, move along the hillside, crossing a small boulder field. Due to a recent re-routing of the trail, the shelter is no longer on the main trail. To locate it, look for a clearly defined junction approximately 0.5 km (0.3 mi) past the bottom of the last climb. This junction is in a scrub forest, approximately 200 - 300 m away from the river; you cannot hear or see the river from the junction. The old trail moves in a downstream direction from the junction towards the river bringing you to the shelter, only about 100 - 150 m from the junction.

Ponderosa Shelter (A.B.)

The Cottonwood

Dominating the river and stream floodplains of the Stein is the stately northern black cottonwood (Populus trichocarpa), a member of the poplar tree family. The cottonwood is dependent on flooding and the deposition of mud since its seeds need a layer of wet mud absent of other plants. This majestic deciduous tree has minimized its energy output for regeneration and greatly enhanced its chances of successful reproduction by matching its seed release with the spring floods. If you hike the Stein's mid-valley in spring, especially from mid-May through June when the river is at its highest, look for the fluffy and sticky buds, which have the distinct odour of balsam.

The cottonwood has adapted to semi-arid environments by using its extensive root system to collect water, and its thick bark and waxy leaves to minimize moisture loss. Come drier times, it is able to survive by restricting fluid flow to its outermost limbs, in essence pruning itself. The cottonwood was important to the Nlaka'pamux. In addition to using it for dugout canoes and smoking fish, they also harvested the sticky buds. The buds were heated and then squeezed to produce a glue for attaching feathers and arrowheads to arrows, and for sealing cracks in canoes.

10. Ponderosa Shelter To Cottonwood Creek

Attractions: Vibrant valley bottom floodplains, the ecological heart of the valley. **Cautions:** Bears frequent the mid-valley in spring and fall; carry water; loose footing in places. **Access:** Depart from Ponderosa Shelter, 21.0 km (13.2 mi) from the Trailhead. **Season:** May - October. **Rating:** Easy to moderate. **Distance and time:** 8.3 km (5.2 mi); 2 - 4 hours. **Elevation gain:** Approximately 150 m (500 ft). **Map:** 92 I/5.

Beaver ponds, large stands of cottonwood, willow thickets, fir, aspen, and abundant birdlife are found on this section of trail. The trail starts immediately west of the shelter. Ponderosa Creek's four channels are soon met, two with small bridges. Caution is needed when travelling through here in spring. 0.4

Spotted owl
(*Strix occidentalis*)
A possible resident of the Stein. (S.W.A.)

km (0.3 mi) past the main channel are rough campsites and a dilapidated log lean-to close to the trail. This is the starting point for those hiking "Victoria Ridge," trip # 30.

Large firs and pine with little ground cover predominate the next 1.0 km (0.6 mi). Little effort is required through this part as the trail is clearly marked and flat. Wet flats and swamp are encountered as the trail takes you close to the river. 1.7 km (1.1 mi) west of Ponderosa Shelter is a rough campsite next to the river with a fire circle and a food rope. Continuing west, swamp predominates again on your left. Pass through a large section of blowdown before levelling off for easy hiking through flat, open fir forests.

Soon, you will pass another swampy area. Those with patience and time may find this area to be good for wildlife observation. Past the swamp is a group of culturally modified trees, primarily cedar, just past a fallen fir you must pass beneath. 1.1 km (0.7 mi) of clear trail leads to drier terrain with dense forest cover. Exercise caution as you cross the boulders above the swamps further along. A great view of the valley, peaks, and floodplains is found atop the outcrops called "Swamp Bluffs." You are now 4.2 km (2.5 mi) from Cottonwood Creek and 4.1 km (2.5 mi) from Ponderosa Creek.

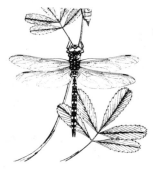

Dragonfly
(order Odonata)
Come summer, the swamps, ponds, and streams of the Stein's mid-valley come alive with the frenzied flying of dragonflies. These insects of ancient design-they date back 350 million years - can be easily observed where the trail comes close to the swamps and ponds between the lower cable crossing and Cottonwood Creek. (R.B.C.M.)

The floodplains of the mid-valley are home to many animals, including the mule deer (look closely) in this picture (D.M.)

The trail quickly drops back to the wet flats. Avoid an old trail to the right, just past the viewpoint. A peaceful river full of colours and life is then encountered as you come alongside the Stein. The next 3.5 km (2.2 mi) of trail is away from the river, offering enjoyable hiking through flat, open forest. Burnt Cabin Creek and a rough campsite with a few tent sites and food rope is your next reference point. Large marshes and swamps occur again on the river side of the trail as you continue through stands of cottonwood, fir, and poplar. An old trail climbing uphill to the right is soon encountered; avoid this and stay on a basically level trail. The remaining 1.2 km (0.8 mi) take you through more flats and past a boulder-strewn hillside. Move alongside the hillside while crossing over the boulders.

The junction with the Blowdown Pass trail is the next marker. Those wanting access to the Cottonwood Basin will use this well-cleared and marked trail. Another 80 m (270 ft) brings you to the Cottonwood campsite on the creek's east bank, which has several tent sites, a food loft, and a fire circle. Excellent views of the valley are found in this area. Cottonwood Falls and a viewpoint 150 m above the valley bottom are well worth the effort. To find the falls, proceed upstream for approximately 10 minutes, moving along the creek's east bank. The viewpoint, about 30 minutes from camp, is located on a ridge just east of the falls and can be reached via the Blowdown Pass trail.

11. Cottonwood Creek to "Logjam Camp"

Attractions: Mid-valley forest bottoms and their accompanying wildlife; easy hiking; refreshing Scudamore Canyon. **Cautions:** Bear country. **Access:** From Cottonwood Creek camp. **Season:** April to October. **Rating:** Easy to moderate. **Distance and time:** To Scudamore Creek, 3.5 km (2.2 mi); 45 minutes - 1 hour 30 minutes. To "Logjam Camp," 8.4 km (5.3 mi), 2 - 3 hours. **Elevation gain:** minimal. **Maps:** 92 I/5 and 92 J/8.

This easy hike takes you through the Stein's flat valley bottom. Scudamore Creek's canyon makes a fine lunch stop or destination on hot summer days.

To cross Cottonwood Creek, follow the orange markers downstream from the campsite, moving along the river bank most of the way. At the time of writing, the only dependable crossing is a crude log bridge. Be careful when crossing, especially during the spring runoff.

American dipper
(Cinclus mexicanus)
A year-round resident of the Stein, the dipper is common along fast-flowing creeks and rivers. It can be seen diving into the water in search of aquatic larvae, snails, and tiny fish. Dippers continually do what appears to be partial deep-knee bends. This unusual movement may possibly be some form of communication between mates. (L.V.E.C.)

Cottonwood Creek with Cottonwood Canyon in the background (I.M.)

The trail is not clear on the west side of the creek. Proceed upstream parallel to the creek, following the orange markers. Only 0.2 km (0.1 mi) from the crossing, the trail turns west (left), away from the Cottonwood. While not entirely clear, the trail can be found by looking for trail markers. A flat and clear path soon emerges from the boulders and logs.

Moving westward, away from Cottonwood Creek, the vegetation changes noticeably, as more undergrowth covers the flat forest floors. The Stein River is approximately 1.0 km (0.6 mi) away and will not be rejoined until west of Scudamore Creek. 1.2 km (0.7 mi) past Cottonwood Creek is a small, seasonal stream. Flat and easy trail conditions continue to be the norm for the next 0.6 km (0.4 mi) except for one short ascent and descent.

Just west of the ascent, 2.1 km (1.3 mi) from Cottonwood Creek and 1.4 km (0.8 mi) from Scudamore Creek, is a small dependable stream. Scudamore Creek's roar is soon evident and accompanies you to the cable crossing. Just 0.3 km (0.2 mi) before the crossing is a collapsed trapper's cabin and campsite with numerous tent sites, a food rope, fire circle, and easy access to water. The cabin was probably occupied between 1920 and 1940, possibly part of an unconfirmed homestead. The trail quickly moves next to the creek and moves upstream parallel to the Scudamore. A short climb brings you to "Rowat Crossing," named for Dr. Nona Rowat of Vancouver, who financed the construction of the crossing. You are now 3.5 km (2.2 mi) from Cottonwood Creek.

Scudamore Creek is also known as Battle Creek, in memory of the last battle between the Nlaka'pamux and Lillooet peoples in about 1830. The murder of a Lillooet man by Nlaka'pamux at a potlatch near present day Hope in the 1770s resulted in a series of conflicts between the two nations. The final battle at Scudamore Creek saw a returning group of Nlaka'pamux convincingly beaten by the Lillooet. A peace pact was made in 1850, restoring the normally peaceful relations between them.

A well-defined trail starts at the west end of the cable crossing platform. For 0.5 km (0.3 mi) you wind through blowdown while moving downhill towards the Stein. The trail soon flattens out and enters denser forest. Approximately five minutes more hiking brings you close to the river and at the base of a small hill. Avoid the numerous game trails on the

No Tree Should Be Without....

Another unseen but vital relationship within forests is found beneath the forest floor. Here the fungi's mycelium - networks of thread-like hyphae - and tree roots work together. The fungi help the tree by extracting moisture and nutrients from the soil, while the tree provides sugar to the fungi. This symbiotic relationship is, in fact, common to all but a few flowering plants. Without this assistance, trees would be small "shrubs," not much larger than a Christmas tree. Fortunately for most trees, dozens of different fungal species are potential partners, ensuring that one fungus is always available. The only evidence we see of this underground work, are the spore laden fruiting bodies (carpophores or mushrooms to most people) by which fungi reproduce. Under the soil, the spores are in the form of truffles, which are distributed on the surface when dug up by rodents, furthering the spread of the fungi.

Cougar
(*Felis concolor*)
(N.W.P.S.)

hillside and proceed to move along the side of the hill. You quickly come to an opening in the trees, offering a great view of the slow, meandering river and peaks to the south. The trail becomes more undulating as you move closer to the river.

Another flood plain soon appears on the left side of the trail next to the river. You are now 1.6 km (1.0 mi) from Scudamore Creek. Flood plains, windfall, and cedar groves dominate the rolling terrain for the next 3.3 km (2.0 mi). You will never move further than a few hundred metres from the Stein in this section. "Logjam Camp," which you will discover is appropriately named, is situated next to the river at a large bend in the river, near the confluence of Nesbitt Creek and the Stein. The deep, dark profile of Nesbitt is visible from camp. A food rope and rough tent sites are found here.

Note: If you insist on having a fire, make camp on the sand and gravel bar west of camp, which can be reached by crossing a small section of backwater; the soil at the main camp is very susceptible to fire! Take the time to look at the large spruce log at the crux of the logjam. It is possible to cross to the opposite bank via the logjam, but exercise caution.

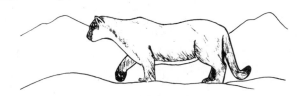

In Search of a Real Male

Cougars, unlike most other mammals, breed year round. Male cougars often follow and fight for the mating role with the desired female. And then they must perform. As with the other large cats, mating is strenuous (the copulation rate is as high as 50-70 times in a 24 hour period!). Why this extreme vigour? Biologists believe that the female assesses the calibre of her potential mate through this high energy process. If she is to produce a large number of healthy young, she requires the finest male available to ensure that her offspring will be strong. A high copulation rate may be part of the criteria she uses in selecting her male partner.

The Deer Mouse

One of the more interesting relationships forest ecologists have discovered is the role of rodents in the regeneration of forests. One such creature you will inevitably meet on an overnight visit to the Stein is the deer mouse. While rodents do hinder the regeneration of a forest by eating many of the tree seeds, they also unknowingly assist the forest. Deer mice and other rodents regularly inoculate the soil by digging up truffles. These underground fruiting bodies of fungi have spores that grow new mycelia (the underground component of fungi), which are essential to the growth of trees (see **No Tree Should Be Without...p.74**). While eating a truffle the mouse inevitably drops a few pieces on the ground, making viable spores of fungal inoculum available for the soil. The consumption of the truffle also has delayed benefits. By defecating throughout the forest as they search for food, deer mice spread the still live truffle spores, and companion nitrogen-fixing bacteria and yeast propagules (another fungus) that pass through their intestines after eating truffles. This process is of considerable importance to the fire-regenerated pine and fir forests of the Stein. The heat of a fire often destroys much of the spore inoculum, bacteria, and fungi in the soil. By making these valuable tree growth assistants available to the seeds that fall in a recently burned forest, the mice help the process of regeneration.

12. "Logjam Camp" to "Lookout Camp"

Attractions: Isolation; lush valley bottoms. **Cautions:** Flooded sections in spring; frequented by bears - make noise when hiking; uneven terrain through boulder fields. **Access:** From Logjam Camp. **Season:** May to October. **Rating:** Moderate. **Distance and time**: To "Grizzly Creek," 4.9 km (3.1 mi); 1 hour 15 minutes - 2 hours 30 minutes. To "Lookout Camp," 7.6 km (4.9 mi); 2 hours - 4 hours. **Elevation gain:** 180 m (600 ft). **Maps:** 92 J/8 and 92 J/1.

Western tanager
(Piranga ludoviciana)
This colourful bird looks like a warbler, but it is not. A common resident of forests, the western tanager is about 15 cm long, all yellow with black wings, white wingbars, and a red head (male). Look for this insect-eating bird in treetops and on the ground. (B.C. Parks)

Clearing the Way

Many of the Stein's trails were built under the joint efforts of the Western Canada Wilderness Committee and the Lytton & Mt. Currie Bands. Since 1986, crews of volunteers have cleared windfall, cut trail paths, constructed the cable crossings, marked the trails, and cairned some alpine routes. Leo deGroot, who has been involved in almost all of the trail work, remembers one time in 1986 as being particularly memorable. Having worked continuously for several weeks, Leo, Ken Lay, and Gerry Bloomer were the only people left to complete the trail from west of Logjam Camp to Stein Lake. To make an already arduous task worse, they had only ten days and a diminishing stock of food and supplies.

"We eventually had a pattern whereby one person would route-find, another would run the chainsaw, and the third would clear the cut deadfall, bushes, etc. off the new trail. Often we had very little route picked out ahead of the chainsaw. At one point, I was flagging the route, Ken was right behind me, cutting through the deadfall, when I came to a cliff edge. We had to backtrack and decided to give the scout more of a lead!"

At the newly constructed upper cable crossing they faced an onerous five kilometres of ground with only three days to go. "We ran out of chain oil for the saw so we used the rest of the cooking oil in the saw. Our food stock was also running low; for dinner one night we had plain macaroni. Breakfast consisted of water-fried bannock (doesn't work well) topped with huckleberries. Now without oil for the chainsaw, we had to dip the bar in water every few minutes to cool it down. This worked, but was more time-consuming. Nevertheless, we had the trail to Stein Lake by 1:30 p.m. July 23, a half hour before the helicopter was due in. The helicopter was three hours late, but that didn't matter as it came complete with a warm pizza!"

Coyote
(*Canis latrans*)
Few animals can match the elusive coyote for adaptability and "street smarts." (N.W.P.S.)

This trail offers a great variety of terrain, vegetation, and views. After travelling westwards through forest for approximately 1.0 km (0.6 mi), you rejoin the river. A boulder field must then be crossed. Look for the trail here as it is not obvious. The trail continues next to the river and remains relatively flat. Cross blowdown and then climb a small hill. Look for orange markers when in doubt.

After crossing a boulder field you move back into the forest again. A cottonwood log-walk follows. 3.8 km (2.4 mi) from "Logjam Camp," you arrive next to the river having walked through the drier, more open forest of Raven Flats. A steep climb up the hillside follows as you move away from the Stein. The trail then levels off with considerable windfall close at hand. Pass through a cedar forest before moving back to the river. "Grizzly Creek" is soon met.

The remaining section of trail to "Lookout Camp" takes you into the Stein's upper canyon, as you climb above the river and gain great views of the valley. The river's pace quickens noticeably as you proceed along the trail and climb above the narrow granitic-rock lined upper canyon.

The trail is in close proximity to the river as you move upstream. A helicopter pad clearing on the opposite side of the river is visible 0.6 km (0.4 mi) from "Grizzly Creek." Some rougher terrain is encountered as you move through wind-blown trees and small boulders. Not until 1.9 km (1.1 mi) from "Grizzly Creek" does the trail climb considerably. The trail soon levels off before becoming more uneven. An enjoyable log walk comes up - careful when wet! Past here the trail is clear and well-marked.

Fabulous views of the canyon and peaks to the west are to be enjoyed after climbing a steep hill that brings you to "Lookout Camp." This camp has a food rope, fire circle, and reliable water at the base of the slopes on its east side.

**Calypso orchid/
Lady's slipper**
(Strix varia).
This is one flower you will not forget. Its pink-purple petals and bright yellow stamens with black tips make it one of the most attractive flowers found in shaded forests. This orchid is 10-15 cm tall and has one green leaf on the base of its reddish stem. (N.B.)

13. "Lookout Camp" to "Avalanche Creek"

Attractions: Scenic upper canyon. **Cautions:** Rough trail with loose footing in places. **Access:** From "Lookout Camp." **Season:** Mid-May to September. **Rating:** Moderate to difficult. **Distance and time:** 2.1 km (1.3 mi); 1 hour - 1 hour, 45 minutes. **Elevation gain:** 150 m (500 ft). **Map:** 92 J/1.

Yes it's a jungle out there (F.S.)

Rougher sections of trail and more demanding terrain are encountered as you leave "Lookout Camp." The next 8.0 km (5.0 mi) of trail to the upper cable crossing are the most demanding of the traverse's valley-bottom trails.

Soon after leaving camp you begin to climb steeply. Look for orange markers and avoid old game trails. You will continue to move along the northern slopes of the upper canyon, approximately 200 m above the river. The trail then levels off into a dry scrubby forest. Fabulous views of the south ridge's glaciers and peaks to the southwest are visible here. Descend and sidehill. The pace is slower due to the rough terrain.

1.5 km (0.9 mi) from "Lookout Camp" is a log crossing that is both enjoyable and nerve-wracking for those not accustomed to such crossings. Careful when the log is wet. More of the same terrain and vegetation as you approach "Avalanche Creek." As you get close to the camp, the vegetation opens up and the trail levels off. "Avalanche Creek," which will have to be forded, is 2 minutes west of camp. A food rope, fire circle, tent sites, and great views are found here. Rumour has it, from the days of trail construction crews, that boot-chewing rats, underwear stealing martens, and chainsaw oil thieving bears prowl this seemingly innocent camp.

14. "Avalanche Creek" To Upper Cable Crossing

Attractions: Great views; enchanting cedar - hemlock forest.
Cautions: Boulder crossing; flooded sections in spring; pack
water. **Access:** From "Avalanche Creek" camp. **Season:** Late
May to September. **Rating:** Moderately difficult. **Distance
and time:** 6.2 km (3.9 mi); 2 hours 15 minutes - 3 hours 30
minutes. **Elevation change:** Descent of approximately 105 m
(350 ft). **Map**: 92 J/1.

Indian paintbrush
(*Castilleja spp.*)
15 - 60 cm high and
red in colour. The
flowers are of differ-
ent colours, but are
hidden by crimson
bracts - similar to leaves
- that give Indian
paintbrush its distinct
appearance.(B.C.
Parks)

Your trip above the upper canyon continues for another 3.0
km (1.9 mi) before you begin to descend towards the valley
bottom. The first 1.6 km (1.0 mi) from the "Avalanche Creek"
camp, elevation 1050 m (3500 ft), is tiring with some elevation
gain over rough, rolling terrain. Approximately 1.6 km
(1.0 mi) from "Avalanche Creek" camp, another camp with a
food rope, water, and rough tent sites is found. A beautifully
situated camp, but beware - the bushy-tailed wood rats here
are cunning and ruthless. "Rat Camp" is an appropriate name.
You have been warned.

The trail moves up and down as you continue westward.
Great views of the peaks and glaciers to the southwest reward
you for your efforts. At approximately the 2.8 km (1.8 mi)
mark, a boulder field is encountered. This can be a little
confusing for travel. The route through this section angles

Looking west from Lookout Camp (N.B.)

Devil's club

(*Oplopanax horridus*)
The name sums up this plant's character. Easily distinguished by its spine-covered stems and large maple-like leaves. Devil's club stands 1 - 2 m tall and is common in cedar groves and other damp and shady places. This plant will reoccur in your nightmares for years if you are unfortunate enough to bushwhack through it.

towards the river as you cross the boulder field; just over half way along the field, heading west, the trail/route drops straight down into the forest below. Look for orange markers and tape. Those coming from west to east should not encounter the same problems, but keep in mind to angle upwards to the top northeast corner of the boulder field in order to find the "groomed" trail.

Continuing in a southwest direction, the trail drops from about 1050 m (3500 ft) to 945 m (3150 ft) through forested slopes. The going is relatively easy and should present no route-finding problems. Exactly 4.0 km (2.5 mi) past "Avalanche Creek" you will find a log crossing over a stream fed by lakes on the North Stein Ridge far above.

Wetter terrain accompanies the flatter valley bottom trail as you continue in a southwest direction. Enjoyable camping next to the river is found 1.8 km (1.1 mi) from the upper cable crossing. Named "Island Camp" by the trail construction crews, this spot has a food rope and is recommended. The remaining 1.8 km (1.1 mi) is straight forward as you continue alongside the Stein's north side, travelling through a variety of vegetation and landscapes. Camping is possible at the upper cable crossing.

15. Upper Cable Crossing to Stein Lake

Attractions: Ecologically rich coastal hemlock forest; great views; bat watching. **Cautions:** Bear country; loose footing on some sections; log crossings slippery in wet weather. **Access:** From the south side of the upper cable crossing. **Season:** Late May to September. **Rating:** Moderate. **Distance and time:** 4.3 km (2.7 mi); 1 hours, 15 minutes - 2 hours. **Elevation gain:** 60 m (200 ft). **Map**: 92 J/1.

With the exception of one or two areas, this section of relatively level trail is clearly visible and presents no problems. The large cedar forests make hiking much more enjoyable on hot summer days. Rolling terrain predominates for the first 2.8 km (1.7 mi).

Having crossed to the south side of the Stein, you soon climb up a steep hillside covered with western white pine and Douglas fir to a wonderful viewpoint offering many photographic opportunities. To the north is the North Stein; Raven Flats and the upper canyon are visible to the east.

Proceed to sidehill, crossing moss-covered boulders as you continue westward passing through one of many cedar groves. A large, solitary boulder is passed 1.2 km (0.8 mi) from the cable crossing. Rolling terrain interspersed with occasional cedar groves predominate for the next 1.6 km (1.0 mi) At this point, you should be at the base of a hill, at the top of which is an excellent view of the North Stein and the main valley to the east. You are now 2.8 km (1.8 mi) from the cable crossing and 1.5 km (0.9 mi) from Stein Lake.

Continuing towards Stein Lake, descend from the viewpoint and proceed to sidehill and descend through what can be a confusing hillside. Eventually, you are back to rolling terrain. 0.6 km (0.4 mi) from the viewpoint is the first channel of Elton Creek. It and the other channels have either log crossings or can easily be jumped. More rolling terrain with some uneven footing brings you to the Stein Lake campsite on the lake's south side, just east of the logjam. A food rope and easy access to the lake are found here but there are few tent sites.

Hiking along one of the pine needle covered trails of the Stein (N.B.)

Winging it

One of the more populous and yet rarely seen group of mammals in the Stein are bats (order Chiroptera). These often maligned creatures of the night can frequently be found over water bodies in pursuit of flying insects; the logjam at Stein Lake is perhaps the best viewing site, hosting several dozen bats when insects are abundant.

The most distinguishing feature of bats is their wings, which are basically arms with enormously elongated forearms and fingers. The airlift necessary for flight is made possible by a skin which extends out to the finger tips and back past the forearm to the knee or ankle. The bats found in the Stein weigh 5 - 20 g and have a wingspan ranging from 25 - 45 cm.

Perhaps the most fascinating attribute of these essentially blind creatures is their navigational system, called echolocation, a process similar to sonar. While flying, a bat emits through its nose or mouth a continuous series of high frequency squeaks - inaudible to the human ear - that reflect off objects and return to the bat's ears. The brain then interprets the information for distance and direction and forms an image of the surroundings.

The bats' hectic midnight feeding frenzies (up to 500 insects an hour!) are an entertaining showcase of their highly effective navigation system and dexterous flight. Moths, beetles, mayflys, and mosquitoes, to name but a few, are normally caught directly in the mouth and less frequently on the wing (literally). Some large insects may be transferred to a tail pouch for later eating. Come autumn, reduced insect populations and colder temperatures mean that some bats such as the silver-haired bat (Lasionycteris noctivagans) migrate south, while others such as the more common little brown bat (Myotis lucifugus) and big brown bat (Eptesicus fuscus) hibernate for the winter. The accumulated fat layers of summer - up to one third of their normal body weight - enable bats to survive until spring while sleeping in confined underground colonies. During hibernation, bats undergo a dramatic transformation as their heart rate slows to about 25 beats per minute (it is normally 400 per minute and over 1000 in flight!) and their temperature cools from 36 - 41° C to approximately 6 ° C. This regime appears to serve bats well, since many of them live as long as 30 years.

"Never doubt that a group of thoughtful, committed citizens can change the world; indeed, its the only thing that ever has."

Margaret Mead

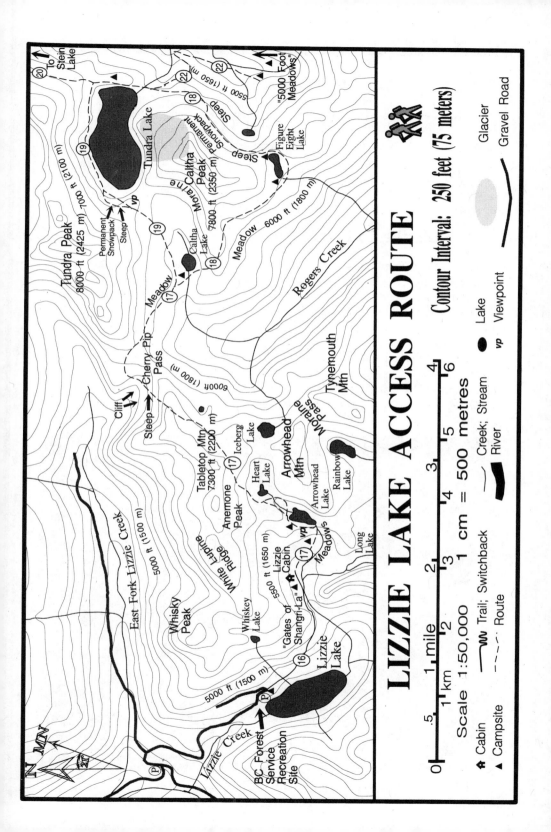

LIZZIE LAKE ACCESS ROUTE

Contour Interval: 250 feet (75 meters)

Scale 1:50,000   1 cm = 500 metres

Cabin
Campsite
Lake
vp Viewpoint
Creek; Stream
River
Trail; Switchback
Route
Glacier
Gravel Road

LIZZIE LAKE TO STEIN LAKE

The alpine between Lizzie Lake and Stein Lake offers some of the most attractive scenery and hiking to be found in the Stein. The terrain is demanding, however, and the weather is volatile at best. Be prepared for weather of all kinds when visiting this area.

Ecological overview: The mountainous terrain between Lizzie Lake and Stein Lake is predominantly alpine tundra. This zone is characterized by several types of vegetation cover, including heather meadows, sedge marsh, and lichens.

16. Lizzie Lake to Lizzie Cabin

Attractions: Enchanting old-growth forest; accessible alpine meadows. **Cautions**: Unpredictable weather; muddy terrain - proper footwear recommended. **Access**: From Lizzie Creek Road, at north end of lake. **Season**: June - September. **Rating**: Moderate. **Distance and time**: 3.0 km (1.9 mi); 1 hour 15 minutes - 3 hours. **Elevation gain**: 285 m (950 ft). **Map**: 92 J/1.

A popular recreation area, the Lizzie Lake - Lizzie Cabin subalpine - alpine sees an interesting mix of motor-bound car campers and backpackers. The alpine area around the Lizzie cabin offers many long week-ends worth of exploration. See Bruce Fairley's *Climbing & Hiking in Southwestern B.C.* for more information on this area. Camping sites are located near the lake's edge.

Passing through the Gates of Shangri-la (G.F.)

Lizzie Cabin (N.B.)

The hardest part of this trip is finding the start of the trail! The perpetual windfalls (hmmmm, do the adjacent clear-cuts have anything to do with this?) often obscure the trail. From the parking lot move towards the lake along a rough trail and take a left after approximately 90 m (300 ft). Proceed to move over, under, and through windfall, avoiding trails on your right for the next 120 - 180 meters (400 - 600 ft). At first you will move away from the lakeshore and then travel parallel to it, once past the windfall, approximately 0.6 km (0.4 mi) from the beginning.

The trail begins to climb at this point. Several streams and muddy sections will be crossed as you continue to ascend from the lake at 1305 m (4350 ft) to the cabin at 1590 m (5300 ft). The gain in elevation brings a thinning of vegetation and occasional glimpses of the lake below. Be sure to check out the Englemann spruce through here. About 1.6 km (1.0 mi) (1 hour - 1 hour 30 minutes) from the start, the trail levels off at approximately 1590 m (5300 ft) and you soon come to a boulder field within close proximity to the creek. You are now 0.8 km (0.5 mi) from the cabin.

Moving along, the slopes on your left steepen and meet the rock slopes from the south to form the "Gates of Shangri-la." To many, this point is like a doorway to another world. The remainder of the trip follows alongside the creek's north bank and crosses rock slopes for 0.2 km before entering open forest. Numerous camping sites are found near the Lizzie Creek Cabin, which was built in 1968 by Tom Anderson, G. Richardson, M. Juri, and D. Nickerson, using their own funds. The cabin is open to the public; please show respect for the cabin and its belongings.

White-tailed ptarmigan

(Lagopus levcurus)
The white-tailed ptarmigan is a fixture of most alpine areas. Its excellent camouflage is attributable to its spotted brown and white plumage, which turns all white come winter. It is able to sustain itself in the harsh alpine environment by feeding upon insects, flowers, buds, and seeds. (F.S.)

17. Lizzie Cabin to Caltha Lake

Attractions: Great alpine scenery; accessible peaks. **Cautions**: Volatile weather; poor footing in the meadows and on the boulders in wet weather; pronounced fog in poor weather. **Access**: From trail starting immediately east of the cabin. **Season**: Mid-July - September. **Rating**: Moderate - difficult. **Distance and time**: To Caltha Lake, 7.2 km (4.5 mi); 6 hours 30 minutes - 10 hours. To Tundra Lake, 8.4 km (5.2 mi); 7 hours 30 minutes - 11 hours. **Elevation gain**: To base of Tabletop Mtn., about 390 m (1300 ft); to Caltha Lake, 195 m (650 ft); to Tundra Lake, 360 m (1200 ft). **Accumulative elevation change**: To Caltha Lake, 705 m (2350 ft); to Tundra Lake, 870 m (2900 ft). **Map**: 92 J/1.

Those wanting to set foot in the Stein, but not able to go further, will find this trip to be worthwhile. Strong hikers can make the round trip in a day, but beware, the terrain is demanding and the weather can change quickly.

Immediately to the east of the cabin a trail begins, quickly taking you across the main channel of the creek. Several trails now appear, most of which proceed in a southerly direction towards the small hill south-southeast of the cabin. The trails quickly flatten out as you come onto a meadow- covered basin, which offers suitable campsites in the drier times of August and September. Now move in a southeast direction; the outflow from Arrowhead Lake at 1800 m (6000 ft) is your immediate goal. The outflow is obvious on the rockface to the east-southeast of your present position. This route's first boulder field crossing is required to gain the lake. Caution is necessary here in wet weather. The 225 m (700 ft) gain in elevation to the lake from the cabin offers rewarding views to the west.

Once across the outflow, continue along the west side of Arrowhead Lake. At the north end you come to a creek where two options are offered: 1) Move along the north side of the creek or 2) cross it and follow the trail in a southeast direction. The south side is easier and more apparent. The two routes soon meet at a flat spot east of a rock outcrop, which provides rough camping sites.

Advance towards the base of a slope to the northeast that forms the north border of a basin in which Heart Lake rests. The trail is clearly defined and well-cairned. You should now be past the west end of Heart Lake and on a bench above it. To continue, climb more or less straight up in a northerly direction, following cairns, or move along the spine of a ridge lying on a southwest-northeast axis. Either way, you soon come to a well beaten path continuing in a northeast direction.

A bench below Tabletop Mountain is reached at an elevation of 2010 - 2040 m (6700 - 6800 ft). Rogers Creek and Caltha Lake immediately west of the Stein divide are visible from here. Move in a northeast direction along the base of Tabletop, crossing relatively flat, boulder-strewn benches and ridges. The numerous cairns are well-constructed and visible through here and have helped the author more than once in hiking through this area in complete fog.

Soon you begin to drop down to Cherry Pip Pass, 1875 m (6250 ft), situated between the east fork of Lizzie Creek to the north and Rogers Creek to the south. From the pass, move in a north-northeast direction towards the base of Tundra Peak. After climbing approximately 90 m (300 ft) to roughly 1950 m (6500 ft) start heading in an east-southeast direction along the boulder-laden slopes of Tundra Peak. Numerous cairns and boulder-hopping here - slow-going for some. Your destination, Caltha Lake, is now 30 minutes - 1 hour away. The grassy meadows and boulder fields you are crossing are home to many marmots and pikas.

Eventually you come onto the rolling meadows north of Caltha. The outflow end of the lake offers the most accommodating camping spots, but be very careful - this is a fragile area. To actually reach the Stein Divide, continue due east and then northeast to the ridge that forms the western boundary of Tundra Lake. The meadows on this approach are open and the going is easy.

Tundra Peak, directly to the north of Caltha, is a moderate scramble for those wishing to gain a good view of the surrounding areas. Ascend from the southeast via a ridge that lies to the west of Tundra Lake. Careful of loose rock. Approaches from the southwest can be frustrating due to the false summit to the southwest of Tundra Peak. Allow a half day for a return trip from Caltha.

Red crossbill finch
(*Loxia curvirostra*)
Identified by its chunky build, short tail, distinctive black crossed bill (which is used to extract seeds of conifer cones), and absence of white wing bars found on similar pine grosbeak and white-wing crossbill. Adult males are varying shades of red; females are yellowish-grey. (R.B.C.M.)

18. Caltha Lake to Tundra Lake via Figure Eight Lake

Black fly
(*Simuliu spp.*, family simuliidae)
What backpacking trip would be complete without a few blood-thirsty insects in constant pursuit? These 2 - 4 mm long flies, often black in colour, are found in the western reaches of the Stein. (M.M.)

Attractions: Great views of alpine and Rogers Creek; remoteness. **Cautions**: Volatile weather; loose and slippery rock. **Access**: From Caltha Lake's west side. **Season**: Mid-July to September. **Rating**: Difficult. **Distance and time**: To Figure Eight, 4.7 km (2.9 mi), 2 hours 30 minutes - 4 hours 30 minutes; to Tundra campsite, 12.2 km (7.6 mi), 6 - 10 hours. **Elevation gain**: 105 m (350 ft). **Accumulative elevation change**: Approximately 405 m (1350 ft). **Map**: 92 J/1.

This route takes you to the Stein Divide via fairly rugged terrain for the average hiker. A shorter, less scenic alternative to this route is to hike along the north shore of Tundra Lake (trip #19). The Figure Eight route is more demanding due to its greater length, requisite route-finding, and steeper terrain.

Cross the outflow at the west end of the lake. Moving south, aim for the west side of the first rock bluff/outcrop and then in a southeast direction across the rock. You then pass a small rock outcrop before coming to level terrain and then past another outcrop to the south. Diagonally cross the next slope in a southwest direction and proceed south across meadow-covered slopes. You should now be at an elevation of 1950 m (6500 ft). Views of peaks to the south are gained from here.

Figure Eight Lake (A.B)

Having left the small meadows, move south, then southwest as you climb along the well-cairned hillside. You should now be moving in a southeast direction at approximately 1950 m (6500 ft), an elevation which must be maintained. Cross a boulder field before moving towards a small valley to the east-southeast. Several small ridges will be ascended as you continue in a southeast direction at 1950 m (6500 ft). The final section before Figure Eight Lake is more difficult as you come to a ridge north of the divide that houses Figure Eight Lake. Here you must move in an east-southeast direction (the target, the divide to the east, is obvious from here). Soon you are at the lake's western outflow where several rough campsites can be found.

To continue to the east side of Tundra Lake, move along the south side of Figure Eight Lake its east end, crossing the permanent snow pack and rock next to the lakeshore. Move up the lake's north side, aiming for Caltha Peak to the north. Your immediate objective is to get above the steeper sections of the south-facing slopes of Caltha Peak you are about to cross, as you begin hiking in a northeast direction. Care is needed as you move to the slope via a rocky ridge. Avoid going low since there are steep slopes leading to the tarn below. Once again you want to move along at approximately 1950 m (6500 ft). Several small snowfields are met as you move across the face towards the ridge that runs east of Caltha Peak. Exercise extreme caution when crossing the snowfields in this area in the morning. If the snow is frozen it makes for treacherous travel and possible fatal results with the cliffs below.

Approximately 2/3 - 3/4 across the face you should be directly underneath a large bluff. Start angling downwards here towards the small ridge to the east. Move through the bushes and trees at the ridge's bottom (avoid going below here since it steepens considerably), and continue moving at your new elevation of approximately 1860 m (6200 ft). You are now 1 hour 30 minutes - 2 hours from the south shore of Figure Eight and 1 hour 30 minutes - 3 hours from Tundra Lake.

The remaining section can be confusing, requiring some route-finding. Again angle towards the next grouping of tree and bush, erring on the low side. You soon come to a pronounced boulder ridge directly to the north, whereby you are below the glacier on the north side of Caltha Peak. Numerous streams and moraine with steepish sections make the next part

Hoary marmot
(*Marmota caligata*)
Look for these bushy-tailed alpine residents sun-bathing on the boulders of their colonies. (N.B.)

**Mountain huckle-
berry/ mountain
bilberry**

(*Vaccinium
membranaceum*)
This densely branched,
coarse shrub is found on
mountain slopes and in
the subalpine. Leaves: 2
- 5 cm long. The purplish-
black berries were har-
vested by native people
both as a food and as a
purple dye. (R.B.C.M.)

difficult. Continue sidehilling at about 1860 m (6200 ft) in a
northwest direction towards the little gully where a creek runs.
Past this, more of the same before the small boulders give way
to the meadows on the southeast side of Tundra Lake, adjacent
to the main outflow. The main campsites are on the ridge north
of the outflow. Descend to and jump across the outflow. An
ascent of 90 m (300 ft) up the ridge brings you to the campsites.
Fabulous views and an undeniable sense of isolation rewards
those making it this far. Water is obtained from the snowpack
and tarns close by. Be very careful in this place; already the site
is showing the signs of damage from ignorant campers who
have made fires.

19. Caltha Lake to Tundra Lake via North Shore of Tundra Lake

Attractions: Relatively quick travel between Tundra Lake's
east side and Caltha Lake. **Cautions**: Steep snow and meadowed slopes; bouldered lakeshore; loose rock slopes. **Access**:
From the ridge west of Tundra Lake, 30 minutes east of Caltha
Lake. **Season**: Mid-July to September. **Rating**: Difficult.
Distance and time: 2.2 km (1.5 mi); 2 hours 30 minutes - 4
hours. **Elevation gain**: 105 m (350 ft). **Map**: 92 J/1.

This is the shorter, less scenic route to the east side of Tundra
Lake (see trip # 18 for the other route). To begin, gain the ridge
on the western shore of Tundra. You have two options to begin
the traverse: 1) Those wanting to avoid crossing the relatively
steep snowpack below will proceed north up the ridge to 1950
m (6500 ft). Then descend to the lake's northwest corner via
the meadows and boulders. 2) Descend across the permanent
snowpack and steep meadows, exercising special care. Following the stream down may be worthwhile.

Once at the northwest corner, move along the shoreline.
Approximately 0.7 km of boulderhopping brings you to a point
where you must ascend 60 - 90 m (200 - 300 ft) above the lake
in order to avoid a shrub-covered bluff that extends to the
waterline. Continue sidehilling at this elevation as you must
stay above another smaller green bluff in the north-east corner
of the lake. Your elevation should be close to that of the ridge
on the lake's east side, 1890 m (6300 ft) Maintain this elevation
to the northeast corner of the lake, cross a small creek, and then
move south along the ridge to the campsites situated among the
small trees.

20. Tundra Lake to Stein Lake

Attractions: Fantastic ridge walk with views of Stein Lake, Stein's south ridge, and North Stein. **Cautions**: Loose rock and steep slopes; scarcity of water; exposed in poor weather. **Access**: From east side of Tundra Lake. **Season**: Mid-July to September. **Rating**: Difficult. **Distance and time**: To Puppet Lake, 4.0 km (2.5 mi), 4 - 6 hours; to Stein Lake, 10.5 km (6.5 mi), 8 - 11 hours. **Elevation change**: Loss of 885 m (2950 ft). **Accumulative elevation change**: To Stein Lake, 1425 m (4750 ft). **Map**: 92 J/1.

This section of the traverse is demanding to all but the most hardened backpacker. You may want to consider breaking the trip in two, with an overnight stop at Puppet Lake. Be sure to drink plenty of fluids; on the ridge there is only the permanent snowpack and Puppet Lake.

The "normal" approach is to gain the saddle on the east-west lying ridge north of the Tundra Lake camp, elevation 2150 m (7200 ft). Move in a northerly direction up the ridge that is directly north of camp. At about 120 m (400 ft) above Tundra camp, you should be close to the small tarn shown on 92 J/1, elevation 2070 m (6700 ft). From here err on the higher western part of the slope so as to avoid some of the steeper snowfields and rocky slopes. Your immediate goal - the saddle next to the ragged peak above - should be obvious from here. Tank up on water - this is your last chance.

Tundra Lake (L.d.)

You are now 45 minutes - 1 hour from the Tundra Campsite. 15 - 30 minutes of scrambling over loose, steep, rocky slopes brings you to the saddle, elevation 2150 m (7200 ft). Above the saddle is a jagged peak which has a large snowfield on its north side. At this point, perhaps the most dramatic scenery of the traverse is before you as you travel this ridge top.

Alternatively, to avoid the rough, rocky route via the saddle described above and below, you can sidehill to the meadows below the ridge and then easily ascend the ridge just west of Puppet Lake. Start by climbing northward on the same ridge used to approach the saddle. At the tarn shown on 92 J/1 sidehill in a northeast direction, descending to roughly 1800 m (6000 ft). Steep shaley slopes eventually give way to trees and bush, making for slow going. Eventually, the open meadows greet you with easier travel, flower-laden slopes (in season), and easy access to the ridge approximately 210 m (700 ft) above.

Returning to the ridge top description, drop down and then climb up to the next peak, staying on its south side. The remainder of the ridge to the peak west of Puppet Lake is slow going with no obvious route. A 210 m (700 ft) descent via the ridge on the southwest of Puppet Lake is required for those intending to camp at the lake. Suitable sites are found on the outlet end of the lake.

Note: In the event of bad weather or for those wishing to avoid the rough and dry descent/ascent of the ridge's eastern shoulder, consider descending or ascending by moving parallel to Puppet Creek on its east side to roughly 0.3 km (0.2 mi) west of Stein Lake. (Large sections of deadfall west - northwest of Stein Lake may be avoided by moving due east at approximately 1200 m (4000 ft) to the southwest corner of Stein Lake.) From there, move alongside Stein Lake's north shore to the logjam. Count on 5 - 7 hours travel, one way. Keep in mind that this route is bushy, especially in the lower sections, and is more difficult than the standard route via the ridge.

To continue to Stein Lake via the ridge top, the route is obvious. The open ridge top east of Puppet makes for easier travel. Moving east of Puppet Lake, stay on the north side of the next peak's western side and once on top, angle into the next dip in a southeast direction, staying on the south side. Elton Falls and Klackarpun Icefield should be visible to the south at this point. Maintain your position on the south-facing meadows at approximately 1920 m (6400 ft) as you move past the

Western hemlock

(*Tsuga heterophylla*)

A common conifer tree of the Coast but less frequent in the Interior. Identified by its drooping tree tip, small (1 - 1.5 cm long) needles, and 2 cm long cone. (B.C. Parks)

Moving along the ridge top between Tundra Lake and Stein Lake (A.B)

third to last peak on the ridge. Proceed up the western ridge of the second to last peak for approximately 160 m. In this parkland-like terrain, look for orange markers on a tree and a cairn indicating the beginning of the marked trail to Stein Lake. You are now at least 1 hour and 15 minutes from the peak west of Puppet Lake and more than 3 hours from Stein Lake.

Maintain an elevation of 1920 m (6400 ft) while sidehilling along these dry slopes. About 0.5 km (20 - 30 minutes) of travel brings you to within 15 m (50 ft) of the dip between the last two peaks. Scramble up to the gap and then continue sidehilling eastward. Approximately 0.5 km more sidehilling is required to gain a slight shoulder where the trail begins to head downhill at a southeast angle. You will now follow the eastern ridge, being sure not to stray off course to the steep slopes to the south and north. The loose footing and absence of water on this section of trail add to the difficulties.

A descent of 750 m (2500 ft) via switchbacks brings you to a point where the trail partially flattens out and the roar of the North Stein River is apparent. Soon, the trail swings west. The Stein River is no more than 300 m away, for those who are dehydrated at this point. The remaining kilometre to the logjam at Stein Lake requires 20 - 30 minutes travel. A campsite with fire circle and food rope is on the south side, easily reached by crossing the logjam.

STEIN LAKE AREA

The following hiking routes have been included for those wanting a rewarding day-trip from either the Stein Lake or Tundra Lake campsites. Please tread lightly in these areas.

Ecological overview: The Stein's western subalpine and alpine is by far the wettest region of the watershed, receiving up to 200 cm of precipitation annually. Indicative of this high rainfall and snowfall is the coastal western hemlock zone east of Stein Lake. Mature stands of trees in this zone provide excellent wildlife habitat, especially for grizzly bears.

Rufous hummingbird
(Selasphorus rufus)
Look for this dull red (male) bird wherever wild flowers grow, both above and below treeline. Having the fastest metabolism in the bird world, hummingbirds are perpetually on the move in search of flower nectar. (R.B.C.M.)

21. Stein Lake to Elton Lake

Attractions: Spectacular views; fabulous alpine. **Cautions:** Carry water; steep slopes in lower sections can be dangerous - be sure to follow the ridge; exposed in poor weather. **Access:** From Stein Lake campsite on south side of lake. **Season:** Mid-June to September. **Rating:** Moderate. **Distance and Time:** 3 km (1.9 mi), 3 - 5 hours one-way; full-day round trip. **Elevation gain:** 800 m (2650 ft). **Map** 92 J/1.

Spectacular Elton Lake is perhaps the most picturesque lake in the Stein; its Klackarpun glacier backdrop, size, and solitary island make it both beautiful and unique.

Note: As you climb the lower section of the ridge be sure to take note of several reference points to assist you in the descent - to wander off to the east or west of the ridge can be dangerous.

Beginning at the Stein Lake campsite on the south side of the lake, proceed directly up the slopes behind camp, in a southerly direction. Your first goal is to identify the ridge that runs in a northeast - southwest direction from the northeast end of Stein Lake to west of Elton Lake; Elton Creek runs parallel to this ridge on its east side for the lower half of the ridge. 10 - 15 minutes of ascent from the lake should bring you to a point where the ridge is evident. At 1380 m (4600 ft) a second ridge to the east joins this ridge. Make note of it so that you take the correct one on the descent.

Continue ascending as you move in a southwest direction through, around, and over bush and rock. At approximately 1500 m (5000 ft), views of the peaks surrounding Elton Lake become more visible. The slope flattens at about 1800 m (6000 ft), at which point you begin to sidehill in a southeast direction towards what is now an identifiable basin that Elton Lake lies within. This final section is straight forward as you hike across the rolling terrain northwest of the lake.

22. Tundra Lake to 5,000 Foot Meadow

Attractions: The ecologically rich meadows west of Stein Lake; isolation. **Cautions:** Grizzly country; volatile weather. **Access:** From Tundra Lake campsite on east side of lake. **Season:** Mid July - September. **Rating:** Moderate. **Distance and Time:** 5.3 km (3.3 mi); half-day one way, full day round-trip. **Elevation change:** Descent of 350 m (1175 ft). **Map:** 92 J/1.

The objective of this trip, an unusual flat meadow surrounded by glaciated mountains, is well worth a visit. From the Tundra Lake campsite, descend to the outflow of Tundra Lake and continue down on the east side of the creek. Heather soon gives way to granite slabs over which the creek cascades to a small pool 75 m (250 ft) below. Cross the boulder field and ascend a grassy gully directly opposite for about 20 m (75 ft). (Do not try to follow the creek down to the meadow; it drops too steeply.) There is excellent camping in the shade of large whitebark pines near several small ponds. From here climb a snow-filled gully to the south, then begin descending in an easterly direction.

Be careful not to descend any gullies on the north side of the ridge towards the creek until you can clearly see the way down into a small heather basin below. The creek cascades into this basin before splitting into two channels to join the stream from the 5000 foot meadow. (The elevation here is actually 5075 ft, 1550 m.) Walk down to the junction of the two streams, then turn right (southwest) and follow the creek back into the meadow. Stay close to the water's edge until entering the meadow by the remains of a beaver dam, then stay along the drier foot of the hillside.

The stream meanders through the meadow with a drop of only 30 m (100 ft) over 1.2 km (0.8 mi). To the south, mountain streams rush from melting glaciers. Hummingbirds are common here, probably because of the varied flower displays. Several small ponds lie 90 m (300 ft) above the meadow floor at its southern end, set among whitebark pines. Camping here is sheltered, but for fresher water you may prefer to camp by the stream to the southeast.

Beaver
(Caster canadensis)
One of Canada's two national symbols (the maple leaf being the other), the beaver.(N.W.P.S.)

From this point you may either retrace your steps or complete a circuit that offers good views of "Cline" and Skookjim mountains and Stein Lake. To take this circuit, sidehill west from the ponds across a large boulder field to where a cascading creek disappears under the rocks. Hike up along this creek to a bluffy area at 1750 m (5750 ft) and then along the gully on the north side of the slabs (the creek is on the south). This opens out into a cirque with a small lake at 1850 m (6080 ft) which may remain snow-bound until August. The flat ground along the lake outflow, if free of snow, has room for several tents. However, the sun sets very early in this location and cool evenings can be expected, with winds blowing over the divide 150 m (500 ft) above. An alternate camping place is directly above on the divide.

To gain the divide, ascend the 60 m scree gully to the north of the lake into a long draw, usually snow-filled. At the top, pick up the route to Tundra Lake described in trip #18 (p. 124). (You can reach the divide near Figure Eight Lake by climbing out of the draw onto the lip of the cirque, then hiking south to the lake.)

Magnificient Elton Lake (K.O.)

Looking south to Elton Falls from the route between Tundra Lake and Stein Lake (D.T.)

SIWHE CREEK - CATTLE VALLEY

Rarely visited, but certainly worth exploring, the alpine regions accessed from Texas Creek's East Fork and Siwhe Creek (see the Road Access section, fold-out map, and inside-cover map for details) provide fabulous ridge walks, rugged scenery, and dry (relatively speaking), open alpine.

Ecological overview: The dry subalpine and alpine of this area is characterized by two biogeoclimatic zones: Engelmann spruce - subalpine fir and alpine tundra. The open parkland of the subalpine zone is easily identified by clumped Englemann spruce and subalpine fir trees interspersed with meadow, grassland, and heath. An excellent example of this is found in upper Cattle Valley. Most of the terrain is alpine tundra, characterized by herbs, lichens, mosses, and dwarf shrubs.

23. East Fork of Texas Creek to "Brimful Lake"

Attractions: Relatively easy access; open ridge walks; panoramic views of Cottonwood basin; clear trail. **Cautions**: Trail muddy and wet in sections; questionable water until over the pass. **Access**: From East Fork of Texas Creek. **Season**: June to early October. **Rating**: Easy - moderate. **Distance and time**: 6.5 km (4.0 mi); 2 - 4 hours. **Elevation gain**: 380 m (1300 ft). **Map**: 92 I/5.

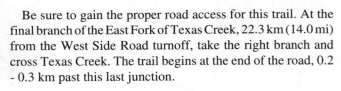

Be sure to gain the proper road access for this trail. At the final branch of the East Fork of Texas Creek, 22.3 km (14.0 mi) from the West Side Road turnoff, take the right branch and cross Texas Creek. The trail begins at the end of the road, 0.2 - 0.3 km past this last junction.

Dusky shrew

(Sorex monticolus)
These primarily nocturnal insectivores are rarely seen, despite their perpetual quest for food. Look for the dusky shrew's small burrows and trails in the snow and amongst the grassy shores of moist areas from valley bottom to alpine. (M.M.)

This unmarked, but clearly visible trail climbs through the forest, crossing several muddy sections with corduroy crossings in the lower section. Ascending from the road at 1730 m (5700 ft) to the pass at 2330 m (7000 ft), you will stay on the East Fork's north slopes. The predominantly subalpine fir forest gives way to meadows and the trail levels out before switchbacking up the boulder-strewn slopes below the pass. The footing can be loose in this section.

Now in the Stein, continue in a southwest direction at an elevation of 2330 m (7000 ft) across rough meadows where the trail remains clearly identifiable. After approximately 0.8 km (0.5 mi), you will begin moving in a southerly direction along the western side of the peak directly north of "Brimful Lake." The rest of the route is straightforward; continue around the peak and move in a southeast direction once past the peak's southwest ridge. "Brimful Lake" should be visible from here. The final section involves a gradual 75 m descent from the shoulder of the ridge and a ramble across the vast meadows to the west side of the lake, where you will find camping sites. Numerous day hikes are possible from the lake, site of the 1985 and 1987 Stein Festivals.

Western anemone
(Anemone occidentalis)
Found in subalpine and alpine meadows, western anemone (tow-head baby) has hairy stems, a fluffy seed head, and a white flower with blue on the outside. This early blooming flower stands 15 - 40 cm in height. (B.C. Parks)

Brimful Lake Trail (N.B.)

24. East Fork of Texas Creek to Stein Divide

Attractions: Stunning alpine; relatively easy access. **Cautions**: Exposed in bad weather; questionable water. **Access**: From East Fork of Texas Creek. **Season**: June to early October. **Rating**: Easy - moderate. **Distance and time**: To meadows, 1.8 km (1.1 mi), 1 - 2 hours; to divide, 2.5 km (1.5 mi), 1 hour 30 minutes - 2 hours 30 minutes. **Elevation gain**: To meadows, 300 m (1000 ft) **Map**: 92 I/5.

A visit to this unique alpine area is well worth the time. If you enjoy open ridge walks, great scenery, and relatively dry alpine, check out this gem of an area. The warmer weather and drier climate of this part of the Stein means that this area is normally accessible earlier in the season than the cooler, wetter alpine to the west.

Finding the beginning of this trail is important. Be sure to follow the East Fork of Texas Creek to its final branch, 22.3 km from the West Side Road turnoff, and take the left hand road of the final branch for another 0.3 km to the trailhead. The right hand road takes you to the "Brimful Lake" trailhead, 0.3 - 0.4 km past the branch.

At the road's terminus you are in a clearcut normally abundant in fireweed (and later in the year, blueberries!). Look for a vague trail that takes you above the road and in a northeast direction for approximately 100 m before starting to switchback up the slopes. Continue up to the southwest corner of the cutblock. Here, at the edge of the forest, is a cascading stream and blue spraypainted markings on the trees. You are approximately 90 m (300 ft) elevation above the road at this point. Past here the trail becomes more apparent.

The trail continues uphill, moving away from the creek in an easterly direction through a beautiful Englemann spruce and subalpine fir forest carpeted with moss and lichen. After roughly 0.5 km (0.3 mi) of relatively easy hiking, the forest opens up and to your right is a small valley, with a moraine on its south side and jagged slopes, elevation 1890 m (6300 ft). You will now travel in an east-southeast direction. Move along the north side of the flat boulder field by following a (usually) wet trail through the meadows adjacent to the boulders. Be sure to stay on the trail so as to minimize your impact on the sensitive meadows.

Indian hellebore
(Veratrum viride)
Found in shady, moist forests from sea level to alpine, Indian hellebore is a tall (1 - 1.5 m), unmistakably tropical-like plant with large ribbed leaves. The greenish-yellow flowers bloom between May and August, depending on the location. All parts of hellebore are extremely poisonous. (B.C. Parks)

Devils Lake

Devils Lake is an area of powerful spirits according to Indian legend. Even today, native people blacken their faces when passing by the lake in order to avoid being recognized by the devil who lives in the lake. One story reported by Judge Thomas Meagher of Lillooet tells of the devil, an old woman with long hair, floating around the lake on a log chanting strange songs. Other accounts tell of herds of goat turning into stone, young maidens dying while swimming, and a bull with a dog on its head attempting to swim the lake and disappearing about halfway across.

After five minutes you begin to climb as the trail gains elevation up the north side of the small valley you are travelling through. Soon the destination should be apparent: The dip in the ridge at the south end of the valley. Open meadows and views of the Stein's southern ridge reward you upon reaching the top, elevation 2070 m (6950 ft). You are now 1 - 2 hours from the East Fork and 30 minutes from the Siwhe Creek - Stein divide. Camping is possible in the meadows surrounding the small tarn in front of you. "Devils Lake," not yet visible, lies in the basin to the south.

To reach the divide, proceed in a southwest direction across the meadows to what should be a clearly distinguishable ridge that connects the meadows you are leaving with the peaks to the south; Siwhe Mountain - the jagged peak that dominates the surrounding summits - is a valuable reference point. From this divide, elevation 1980 m (6600 ft), you can descend down into Cattle Valley or proceed along the ridge to "Earlobe Lake," "Blueberry Hollow," and the Ponderosa drainage, with the option of ridgewalking to Cottonwood Creek's confluence with the Stein (see trips 28 and 29).

25. Siwhe Creek to Stein Divide

Attractions: Scenic canyon; access to "Devils Lake;" good trail with only a few rough sections. **Cautions**: Loose footing on boulder field crossings; questionable water. **Access**: From West Side Road, 26.2 km (17.3 mi) north of ferry. **Season**: Late May - early October. Rating: Moderate. **Distance and time**: About 12.5 km (7.8 mi); full day. **Elevation gain**: 1455 m (4850 ft). **Map**: 92 I/5.

This well-cleared trail is a lengthy but scenic access route to the Cattle Valley alpine normally gained via Texas Creek. The Hance family takes their cattle to (where else?) Cattle Valley via this trail. The lower section of trail crosses the Hance's farm and reserve property; ask permission before parking and crossing their property (from the 24.1 km access point at the sharp switchback on the West Side Road drive 2.5 km north, at which point a rough road leaves the West Side Road and quickly brings you to a gate and house).

Wolf spider
(Pardosa spp.,
family lycosidae)
This 10 - 15 mm long
(body), primarily grey-
brown spider is appropri-
ately named. Being a
ground-dwelling spider,
it does not construct a
web. Rather, it moves
across the forest floor or
rocky slopes in pursuit of
insect prey which it
pounces upon. (M.M.)

Starting at the sharp switchback, enter the fields and move directly north to the visible Siwhe Creek canyon. Measured distances start at the canyon edge. Move west uphill along the banks of the canyon. After 0.3 km (0.2 mi) of easy ascent a road from the south is met. Continue moving alongside the canyon edge via the road, which is above the remains of a flume (wooden water channel). 0.5 km (0.3 mi) from the start, the road ends and a trail continues left up the bank and crosses a foot bridge that spans a steep gully.

90 m past the bridge, the beginning of the dirt water channel is encountered. At this point you are well above Siwhe Creek, which can be heard, but not seen. Avoid a trail on your left 0.3 km (0.2 mi) past the beginning of the water channel and continue along rolling terrain. The next 1.1 km (0.7 mi) has a well-cleared trail that descends into a small gully and eventually to the edge of a clearing. Here is an excellent example of forest succession; the trees are slowly reclaiming this former field. Good views of Siwhe canyon to the west and the Fraser River to the east are found here.

Cross the field in a southwesterly direction to the cabin remains in the southwest corner. Regain the trail behind the cabin with the adjacent barbed wire fence. Move past windfall and resume a roughly parallel route to the water channel. 0.5 km past the cabin is a fork in the trail that may be confusing to those coming downhill on this trail; stay to the right at this fork if descending. The next 0.8 km (0.5 mi) of trail is easily followed as you continue through scrubby forest before descending to the creek. 120 m along the creek is a sturdy bridge that crosses the creek. Avoid this crossing and continue upstream on the south side of the creek. As indicated above, the water from Siwhe Creek is of questionable quality due to the presence of livestock further upstream.

The trail now moves close to Siwhe Creek and begins to ascend more steeply for the next 3.4 km (2.1 mi). 0.5 km (0.3 mi) past the bridge the canyon narrows and then broadens 0.2 km (0.1 mi) further. An easy 0.2 km (0.1 mi) of hiking brings you to a sturdy bridge. Cross here to the north side of the creek. Now sidehill across rocky terrain as the trail continues to ascend, leveling off only briefly 0.2 km (0.1 mi) past the bridge. Brief views of the steep canyon walls above are possible through here. After moving alongside the creek, two boulder slopes with loose footing are crossed before entering a small forested section of trail with an island in the creek below. You are now 4.9 km (3.1 mi) from the start of the trail.

The trail then steepens considerably as it switchbacks four times, climbs, and then switchbacks four more times. More boulder slopes closer to the creek are crossed before a side valley to the south becomes visible, elevation 1290 m (4300 ft). The trail has been measured only as far as here. Beyond this point, 6.9 km (4.4 mi) from the start, the trail continues to ascend in the gradually opening valley. Windfall becomes more pronounced and some confusion is possible given the numerous cattle trails through here. Rough camping sites are found on the north shore of "Devils Lake," elevation 1695 m (5650 ft). The numerous trails through the meadows north of the lake may be confusing when moving between the lake and the Stein Divide to the west. At the divide, you are at the terminus of trip # 24 and at the starting point of trips 26 - 28.

26. Stein Divide to "Brimful Lake" via "Rainbow Ridge"

Attractions: Good views; open ridge walk. **Caution**: Loose footing in places; exposed in bad weather. **Access**: From Siwhe Creek - Stein divide (terminus of trip # 25). **Season:** Late June to early October. **Rating**: Moderate - difficult. **Distance and time**: 6.0 km (3.8 mi); 4 - 6 hours. **Elevation gain**: To the northern slopes of the peak east of Brimful Lake, 165 m (550 ft). **Accumulative elevation change**: 480 m (1600 ft). **Map**: 92 I/5.

This route is an excellent way of gaining views of the alpine and side valleys of the eastern Stein, making a 1 - 2 day round-trip from the East Fork of Texas Creek. Keep in mind that the slopes along the ridge and above "Brimful Lake" are comprised of loose rock and are moderately steep in places.

Start at the terminus of trip # 25, on the Siwhe Creek - Stein Divide, elevation 1980 m (6600 ft), and locate a small peak northwest of the ridge that forms the divide. After a quick 150 m ascent of this peak, proceed in a westerly direction. The route is obvious from here: The ridge lies west and presents no problems. Stay to the south side as you move into the saddle.

Cattle Valley (T.H.)

"Wilderness is a re-
source which can shrink
but not grow. Invasions
can be arrested or
modified in a manner to
keep an area usable ei-
ther for recreation, or
science, or for wildlife,
but the creation of new
wilderness in the full
sense of the word is im-
possible."

Aldo Leopold

Once at the saddle, proceed up the slopes of the next peak, veering to the left of the smooth rock faces. Here you have two options: 1) Move straight up through the Krummholtz to the top, for a 30 m elevation gain. 2) Sidehill at 2090 m (6900 ft) on the south slopes of the peak for approximately 300 m. This route is not obvious but is acceptable, allowing easier access to the ridge top.

You are now 15 - 30 minutes from the peak east of "Brimful Lake." Moving southwesterly up the boulder-strewn ridge, fabulous views of the Cottonwood basin to the east will greet you at the top. From this point, elevation 2280 m (7600 ft) and 60 m (200 ft) below and north of the summit, the lake is easily accessed. Simply sidehill down the west-facing slopes of the peak, angling to the middle of the slopes in a southwest direction, and then in a northwest angle to the lake's northeast corner. Be sure to stay on the northern end of this peak's western slopes - the slopes further to the south are loose and steep. Allow 1 hour - 1 hour 30 minutes for the 285 m (950 ft) descent.

27. Stein Divide to "Brimful Lake" via Cattle Valley Headwaters

Attractions: Great scenery; open alpine; accommodating routes. **Cautions**: Exposed in bad weather; loose rock; carry water. **Access**: From Stein divide (terminus of trip # 24). **Season**: Late June to early October. **Rating**: Moderate - difficult. **Distance and time**: About 5.0 km (3.3 mi); 4 - 6 hours. **Elevation gain**: 390 m (1300 ft). **Accumulative elevation change**: 735 m (2450 ft). **Map**: 92 I/5.

This route makes a round-trip from Texas Creek to "Brimful Lake" and back a possibility. It is not as difficult as the "Rainbow Ridge" route and is arguably more scenic.

This route begins on the western slopes of Cattle Valley's upper meadows. It is important to find the correct slope to ascend - the 1:50,000 map (92 I/5) is essential. Locate "Brimful Lake" on the 92 I/5 map. Directly east of the lake is a peak which has a ridge that extends southeast into Cattle Valley. It is this ridge with a pronounced round top on its east side that you must ascend.

At the 1950 m (6500 ft) elevation level on the round sum-mit's north slopes, begin ascending the meadow-covered slopes in a southerly direction, sidehilling rather than climbing straight up. After 60 - 90 m (200-300 ft) elevation gain you should find the slopes easier to directly ascend. You should now be moving in a westerly direction. About 1 hour from the valley bottom and 285 m (950 ft) higher, you are now atop the round summit. From here, the going is easier. Move in a northwest direction into the dip and ascend the slopes to the west, passing over boulders and bedrock. The 2250 m (7800 ft) peak directly above Brimful rewards your efforts with a great 360 ° view.

To descend to "Brimful Lake," walk directly south to the talus slopes of the ridge connecting the peak you just ascended, dropping 75 - 90 m (250 - 300 ft) over a distance of approximately 300 metres. You are now above moderately steep slopes, which contrary to appearances, are relatively easy to descend. Move in a northwest direction, aiming for the south end of the lake. Allow 20 - 40 minutes for the descent.

Shaping the Land

The majestic, jagged peaks and gentle alpine meadows near Devils Lake are more than just spectacular scenery. Here one also finds many excellent examples of the glacial erosion processes that have shaped the landscape. During the ice ages, the ice sheet covered all but the highest peaks and crests above about 2600 m. The scouring action of the glaciers enlarged cirques (steep-sided, bowl shaped valley heads) and troughs at the expense of lands between the highest points, giving rise to the distinctive, steep-sided peaks (Stein, Siwhe, and Skihist are typical glacial hornes) and ridges (aretes) so prominent today. Ridges and summits below about 2600 m were overridden by ice streams. They are distinguished by their rounded profiles and provide for excellent ridge walks - the ridge north of Earlobe Lake being perhaps the best example in this area. Also easily identified are two of the more obvious cirques in the Stein: Brimful Lake and Earlobe Lake. At each of these cirques the strong scouring action of the glacier's head carved out a deep bowl. The melting of the glacier at each of these cirques resulted in the lakes (tarns) found today.

Mountain goat

(Oreamnos americanus)
This alpine resident is
found on steep, rocky terrain, feeding on grasses.
Pellet-like droppings and
rough game trails on
ridge tops are the most
common signs of these
shy ungulates. (S.W.A.)

28. Stein Divide to Upper Ponderosa Creek

Attractions: First class ridge walk; fabulous scenery; isolation; access to Siwhe and Stein Mtns. **Cautions**: Carry water;
exposed in poor weather. **Access**: From Stein - Siwhe Creek
divide (terminus of trip # 25). **Season**: Late June to early
October. **Rating**: Moderate - difficult. **Distance and time**: To
above Earlobe Lake, 2.5 km (1.5 mi), 1 hour 30 minutes - 3
hours; to lake northwest of "Victoria Ridge," 12.0 km (7.5 mi),
5 - 7 hours. **Elevation gain**: To above "Earlobe Lake," 270 m
(900 ft); to lake northwest of "Victoria Ridge," 30 m (100 ft).
Accumulative elevation change: 1170 m (3900 ft).
Map: 92 I/5.

This route is suitable for a day-trip to "Earlobe Lake" and
persons seeking the remoteness and beauty of the upper
Ponderosa Creek basin. Starting at the divide between Cattle
Valley and Siwhe Creek (terminus of trip # 25), proceed south-
southeast atop the dry, open ridge dividing the two valleys. You
will soon reach the first rise within 15 - 20 minutes of easy
hiking. Stay on the west side of the face while ascending.
Views of "Devils Lake" and the surrounding peaks are found
at the top, a gain of 110 - 120 m (350 - 400 ft).

Continuing along, initially gradual slopes give way to steeper
terrain as you proceed towards "Earlobe Lake." While there are
no problems in route finding or terrain, resist the temptation to
avoid the next small ascent by sidehilling on the west side of
the final small summit to the northeast of Earlobe - the bush and
loose footing of the slopes makes for slow travel. Now 1 - 2
hours from the start and at an elevation of 2130 m (7100 ft), you
are approximately 120 m (400 ft) above the lake. For the most

Brimful Lake 1985 Stein Festival Site (A.D.)

rewarding views, especially of the Stein River and Skihist and Petlushkwohap peaks, continue along the ridge, ascending one small peak, dipping slightly, and then ascending a small summit northeast of "Earlobe Lake."

To continue to "Blueberry Hollow" and the rest of the upper Ponderosa Creek basin, descend from the peak in a southwest direction to the base of the summit directly south of Earlobe. From here the sloping, boulder-strewn meadows of "Blueberry Hollow" can be crossed. Camping sites are found by the lake in the northeast corner of this valley. Moving past "Blueberry Hollow," stay on the west side of the valley, sidehilling around the base of the summits to the west.

Approximately 1.5 km (1.0 mi) of travel brings you to the slopes of the peak more or less west of the aforementioned lake on the east side of the hollow. At these slopes, you begin to "round the corner." The west side of the basin opens up, revealing a small forest to the southwest. Descend in a southwest direction through the meadows, which give way to open forest. You are now 3 - 4 hours from the Stein Divide and 2 - 3 hours from the end of this route. Your goal is the boulder-laden slope below the jagged peaks to the west. Be sure to fill your water bottles at the stream in the forest before climbing the slopes.

You should now be at the base of the talus slopes, at approximately 1950 m (6500 ft), with the jagged peaks above. These peaks form a distinctive ridge along the western boundary of this valley, clearly identifiable on the 1:50,000 map. Ascend the loose and relatively steep slopes to roughly 2100 - 2150 m (7000 - 7200 ft) in a southwest - west direction and then move in a southwest direction. Gain the visible notch in the peaks to the southwest and then proceed along the ridge top, being sure to take the western ridge (an eastern ridge branches off in a southeast direction towards Ponderosa Creek). Atop the summit of this ridge, elevation 2240 m (7400 ft), the goal of this route, Meadow Lake, which lies in the southwest corner of this valley, should be visible. Angle southwest to the saddle between the peak you are on and the summit to the southwest and then descend across the meadows to the lake. Several suitable camping sites are found here, the perfect base for exploring this wonderful pocket of wilderness.

Clark's nutcracker
(Nucifraga columbiana)
This 30 cm long jay has a grey body, black and white wings, and is most easily distinguished from the grey jay by its long black beak, which is used to tear open whitebark pine cones. It is often found in subalpine forests. In the Stein, the area near Blowdown Pass is frequented by several Clark's nutcrackers. (R.B.C.M.)

29. Upper Ponderosa Creek to Cottonwood Creek

Whitebark pine
(Pinus albicaulis)
Found from subalpine to timberline, thriving on rocky, exposed terrain. Easily identified by its high elevation habitat, five needled sheath, and thick cones. (M.M.)

Attractions: Great views; great ridge walk. **Cautions**: Carry water; steep slopes with loose footing in places; route-finding required; some bush. **Access**: From terminus of trip # 28. **Season**: Late June to early October. **Rating**: Difficult. **Distance and time**: 7.5 km (4.8 mi); 4 hours - full day. **Elevation gain**: 240 m (800 ft). **Accumulative elevation change**: 1800 m (6000 ft). **Map**: 92 I/5.

Do not travel this ridgewalk-bushwhack unless you are experienced in route-finding, in good shape, part camel, and have a sense of humor. The rewards of the route are near its beginning - unparalleled views of the Stein River and the alpine regions surrounding the watershed. After this high point (literally!), the route becomes an enjoyable ridge walk in parkland terrain before descending through fir and pine forest. Total elevation loss: 1560 m (5200 ft). Ensure that you have enough water for this dry trip.

If starting out from Meadow Lake at the terminus of trip # 28, proceed directly west to the distinctive meadow-covered face of the summit directly west of the lake; this summit is not as jagged and pronounced as those to the south. Now hike in a northerly direction along the ridge to the highest peak on this western ridge at 2250 m (7500 ft). Some parts of this ridge require moving carefully around jagged rock outcrops. Finally at the top, you are 1 hour - 1 hour 30 minutes from the lake and 240 m (800 ft) higher. If this view does not move you...

From this vantage point, the route to Cottonwood Creek and the Stein River should be obvious. The ridge connecting the peak you are on extends west and then southwest into Cottonwood Canyon. Be sure that this route is clear in your mind before continuing. Loose rock and steep slopes demand slower hiking at first; err on the north side. Once into the first dip with trees atop the ridge, well-defined game trails can be followed on the north side of the ridge, which then flattens out and opens up offering enjoyable rambling with good views. About 2.3 km past the 2250 m (7500 ft) peak and still on relatively open and flat terrain, an important change in the terrain becomes apparent. To continue west is to encounter steep slopes on the eastern side of Cattle Valley Creek. The goal is to connect onto the ridge that descends in a southwest direction towards the lower Cottonwood Canyon.

Before dropping into this forested ridge get a rough target of peak(s) in the distance to use as a reference point. A compass reading is also useful. The first 0.5 km (0.3 mi) is a steep descent down shrub, tree, and blowdown laden slopes, interspersed with a myriad of game trails. Below 1500 m (5000 ft) be sure to maintain your reference points so as to continue in a southwest direction (important!) towards the Cottonwood's lower canyon. The final 450 m (1500 ft) of descent is steep in places. Ideally, you will connect with the Blowdown Pass trail, elevation 960 m (3200 ft), which is situated on the east side of Cottonwood Canyon. From here you are only 45 minutes - 1 hour from Cottonwood camp, elevation 690 m (2300 ft).

30. "Victoria Ridge"

Attractions: The alpine of the Ponderosa Creek basin; great views of Stein Valley. **Cautions**: Drink plenty of water before starting and carry as much as you can; demanding hiking requiring solid route-finding skills. **Access**: From Ponderosa Creek, if ascending, or terminus of trip # 28 if descending. **Season:** June to October. **Rating:** Difficult. **Distance and time**: Approximately 4 km (2.5 mi); 4 - 5 hours one way, a **long** day for a round-trip. **Elevation gain**: 1500 m (5000 ft) **Map**: 92 I/5.

This inconspicuous ridge offers both access and exit from the alpine of the Ponderosa Creek drainage. Be prepared for considerable vertical gain, bush, narrow ridges, and dry conditions. (In other words, this is another route for those with a well-developed sense of humor.) Stop frequently to assess the situation and note landmarks for your descent.

Begin on the western side of the four channnels of Ponderosa Creek at a dilapidated log shelter, just off the main trail. Proceed northwards, staying within 150 - 200 m of the creek for approximately 0.5 km. The terrain quickly steepens as you leave the valley bottom and begin ascending the valley's northern slopes. Your first goal is the lower reaches of the ridge at 1200 - 1500 m (4000 - 5000 ft). The 1:50, 000 map shows a distinct knob at 1350 m (4500 ft), the stopping point for those wanting views of the valley but who are limited for time. At this point, the sheer-sided canyon of Ponderosa Creek is visible.

Proceed now in a northwest direction along this rough ridge, being careful not to venture off to the east or southwest. Old blazes may be found in the denser timber of the narrowing ridge as you continue to climb. Some windfall will undoubt-

Long-tailed weasel
(Mustela frenata)
This primarily nocturnal weasel is found throughout the valley in pursuit of small mammals and birds. Size: 40 cm long. Summer coat is cinnamon brown above and white below. (M.M.)

White-crowned sparrow

(Zonotrichia leucophrys)
Commonly seen in small flocks in most habitats, feeding on the ground searching for insects and seeds. This 15 cm long sparrow is identified by its black-capped head, which has three stripes across it, and greyish breast. (R.B.C.M.)

edly slow your progress. Eventually the forest cover thins out as you move above the 1800 m (6000 ft) level. The summit, 2100 m (7000 ft), is gained by scrambling up the final section of rock. Camping is found at Meadow Lake further northwest along the ridge, less than 1 hour away. Water is most easily obtained by descending north to a small pond. To continue to Cottonwood Creek proceed to the aforementioned lake and then follow trip # 29. Cattle Valley and Texas Creek are reached via trip #28.

A Healthy Appetite

One insect that has recently gained recognition for its appetite is the mountain pine beetle (family Scolytidae). This small (5 - 10 mm long) beetle has dramatic population explosions, resulting in the destruction of large numbers of pine trees. A conflict between two consumers of pine trees - mankind and pine beetles - inevitably ensues.

Weak trees which can be overcome by beetles are usually widely scattered in a healthy forest. Central to the maintenance of healthy pine forests are fires, which normally thin forests, leaving only the strongest trees.

If fires do not occur, however, a portion of the forest may become stagnant. Competition between the trees for nutrients, water, and space is intense, and eventually a closed canopy of dense pine trees develops. At this point, the trees are susceptible to insect infestation.

Pine beetles eventually move into the stagnant forest area and begin to proliferate. The outbreak builds slowly and eventually peaks. When the supply of suitable trees diminishes, the beetle population decreases, the

Earlobe Lake (L.d.)

dead trees fall and decompose to provide nutrients for future forests, and the forest begins a process of regeneration.

Unfortunately, this beetle has become one of the forest service's and industry's favorite excuses for clear-cutting large tracts of forest. The "salvage logging" operations so common in the Interior are based upon the premise that the timber infested by the pine beetles will create fire hazards and otherwise remove valuable timber from industry's pocket book. This perceived threat is based strictly on an economic point of view.

Insect infestations, like other natural disturbances such as disease and fire, are in fact part of the natural cycle. Left alone, the forests will regenerate naturally. One need look no further than the Stein to see forests that have been regularly exposed to these disturbances. Despite these stresses, the forests are doing just fine without man's intervention.

BLOWDOWN PASS - COTTONWOOD BASIN

While somewhat spoiled by a mine access road, the Cotton-wood area has plenty of accommodating terrain. Plus, for those wanting a shorter one-way traverse through the Stein, Blowdown Pass and the road and trails that connect with it allow you to experience the alpine, subalpine, mid-valley forests, and lower canyon of the Stein in a four to seven day trip. **See the Road Access section for a description of the access to Blowdown Pass.**

Red-tailed hawk
(Buteo jamaicensis)
Common in open coun-try, where it can be seen soaring above mead-ows. Gains prey - prima-rily rodents - by gliding down in surprise. A red-tailed will pursue other birds, frogs, salaman-ders, and even fish. The red-pink tail, which is broad in flight, is the best means of identification. (M.M.)

Ecological overview: The Cottonwood Creek drainage en-compasses three of the Stein's six biogeoclimatic zones. Most hikers will access this area via Blowdown Pass , which is in the alpine tundra. The subalpine zone - Englemann spruce - subalpine fir - lies between the alpine and the lower elevation Interior Douglas fir forests, which extend from the valley bottom up Cottonwood Creek to just north of the junction and to an elevation of roughly 1350 m (4500 ft).

31. "Kidney Lakes"

Attractions: Accessible alpine lakes. **Cautions**: Slippery ter-rain when wet. **Access**: From outflow (west) end of Blowdown Lake. **Season**: Early to mid-June to October. **Rating**: Easy - moderate. **Distance and time**: 1.0 km (0.6 mi); 30 minutes - 1 hour. **Elevation gain**: About 30 m (100 ft). **Map**: 92 J/8.

For a short, scenic trip from "Blowdown Lake," this route is worth considering. Move in a southwest direction from the lake's outflow, crossing the meadows which give way to forested slopes and boulder fields adjacent to the ridge you will move along the north side of. Maintain an elevation of 2010 m (6700 ft). You should be close to the prominent northwest pointing extension of the main ridge you are moving alongside. This protrusion, a valuable reference, lies south of "Blowdown Lake" and is visible from the lake.

Talus slopes and boulder fields extend out from the ridge at this point and the forest thickens. Having come around the boulder slopes of the ridge's extension, move in a southerly direction, ascending steepish meadows for an elevation gain of 30 m (100 ft) to the plateau that sits slightly above the small tarns (small alpine lakes). Here at approximately 2040 m (6800 ft) is your destination, several small tarns.

32. North Fork of Scudamore Creek

Attractions: Remote alpine; the scenic North Scudamore; opportunity for numerous day-trips. **Cautions**: A 1:50,000 map is essential; some bushwhacking and loose, rocky slopes; do not attempt in bad weather. **Access**: From outflow (west) end of "Blowdown Lake." **Season**: Late June to late September. **Rating**: Moderate - difficult. **Distance and time**: To lake north of pass, approximately 4.0 km (2.5 mi), 3 hours - 4 hours, 30 minutes; to "Cirque Lake," 6.0 km (3.8 mi), 4 - 6 hours. **Elevation gain**: To pass, about 120 m (400 ft). **Map**: 92 J/8.

The South Blowdown - North Scudamore area is an intriguing subalpine and alpine mosaic of ridges, tarns, meadows, wildlife, and forests. From the outflow of "Blowdown Lake" proceed in a southwesterly direction through the meadows which give way to forested slopes interspersed with boulders, maintaining an elevation of 2010 m (6700 ft). Your first reference point is the outflow from the "Kidney Lakes" (see previous description for access to the lakes). At this point the bush is thick and the slopes steep. The easiest route of travel is to descend to approximately 1890 - 1920 m (6300 - 6400 ft), and then sidehill in a southwest direction, eventually crossing a large boulderfield.

Maintain this elevation except for a quick scramble up one or two meadowed slopes. Open forest with numerous wet sections from small creeks draining melting snowpack above are crossed. Approximately 1.0 km (0.6 mi) of sidehilling brings you to gentler slopes rising to a small plateau nestled against the large ridge you are travelling alongside. Here are several small tarns at 2100 - 2130 m (6800 - 6900 ft) and open spaces - a great lunch spot or camping site in drier months. To reach the lake north of the pass requires 15 - 20 minutes of easy rambling through the meadows.

Pushing on to the not yet visible "Cirque Lake," which lies in the north fork of Scudamore Creek (neither the north Scudamore nor "Cirque Lake" are indicated on the 92 J/8 topo map), the pass requires a climb of 90 m (300 ft) from the lake north of the pass to the pass proper at 2025 m (6750 ft). Your objective should now be visible to the southwest. To descend to "Cirque Lake," 30 minutes - 1 hour away, go to the right of the vegetation-free gully (shown on the 1:50,000 map) and descend through a vegetated gully, bolstered with solid footing. Descend to 1950 m (6500 ft) and then cross the meadows

Meadow vole
(Microtus pennsylvanicus)

Seldom seen, but almost always present in grassy marshes and meadows is this rodent-like creature. The meadow mole is active primarily in the morning and late afternoon feeding on grasses and sedges. Come winter, they live off their stockpile collected during the fall. (B.C. Parks)

The rough ridge top between Cirque Lake and Silver Queen Mine (H.J.)

to the lake. This section can be wet with many streams draining the snowpack until late in the season. At the lake there are several suitable dry campsites - please be careful - this is a fragile area that already bears the scars of ignorant campers. Your imagination is the only limit to possible day-trips from here.

33. "Kidney Lakes" to Silver Queen Mine

Attractions: Fabulous ridge walk; incomparable views of North Scudamore. **Cautions**: Drink lots of water before going and be sure to carry a map; rough terrain with loose footing in places; hike this route in the longer days of June - August. **Access**: From lakes 0.8 - 1.0 km east of the pass between Blowdown and North Scudamore (see route # 32). **Season**: Late June to late September. **Rating**: Moderately difficult. **Distance and time**: About 11.5 km (7.0 mi); full day. **Elevation gain:** 165 m (550 ft). **Accumulative elevation change**: more than 750 m (2500 ft). **Map**: 92 J/8.

This route has not been hiked in its entirety by the author, but it is a feasible route. Thanks to Herb Johnston for assisting with this route description. The starting point for this trip is in Blowdown Creek's southernmost branch, where the "Kidney Lakes" and North Scudamore routes are found. Follow the "Blowdown Lake" to North Scudamore route to the tarns approximately 0.8 km to 1.0 km east of the pass between Blowdown and Scudamore. The tarns lie between 2040 m (6800 ft) and 2190 m (7300 ft) in a distinctly benched area with several broad flat sections. An early start from this spot is recommended.

Your first goal is to climb to the col between the valley you are presently in and the South Fork of Cottonwood - it should be visible to the east-southeast of your position. This route is relatively straightforward as you work around the lakes; be sure to drink a lot of water here and top up your water bottles.

Once at the col, your next objective, the ridge to the south, is apparent. To reach the ridge you must descend 60 - 90 m (200 - 300 ft) to the relatively flat large bench and then move across the bench in a southeast direction for approximately 1.0 km (0.6 mi). This section is comprised of rough, rocky terrain and can be time consuming. A scramble up the ridge's north slopes takes you to the ridge top at 2160 m (7200 ft).

From this point the route is obvious as you follow the ridge top. Stay on the south side of the ridge for the first 2 km, at which point you then descend to the ridge's vegetated low point at 1935 m (6450 ft). At 1980 m (6600 ft) the ridge broadens, followed by a gradual elevation gain of 150 m (500 ft) over approximately 2 km to the 2145 m (7150 ft) peak above the uppermost lake of the Silver Queen Mine area. See the Silver Queen Mine to Stein River route description if in doubt as to how to descend to the lake below; at this point, however, thirst may overtake all rational thought processes.

34. Summit South of Blowdown Pass

Attractions: Most accessible views of main Stein Valley from Blowdown Pass. **Cautions**: Exposed in poor weather; loose footing in places. **Access**: From final bend in road west of Blowdown Pass. **Season**: Mid June to late September. **Rating**: Moderate. **Distance and time**: 1.2 km (0.8 mi); 2 hours round-trip to viewpoint, 3.0 km (1.9 mi), 4 hours round-trip via Kidney Lake return. **Elevation gain**: 270 m (900 ft). **Map**: 92 J/8.

From the final bend in the road west of Blowdown Pass move south up a broad gully to an open snow/boulder field. Excellent views are soon gained from the top of this ridge, with the best vantage point being at the 2400 m (8000 ft) peak. Those wanting a half-day loop trip will continue along the ridge to the steep slope above "Kidney Lakes" and descend to the Lakes. From the "Kidney Lakes," "Blowdown Lake" is only 30 minutes northeast (see Trip # 31 if the route is unclear).

Biological diversity is the wealth of life on earth, the millions of plants, animals, and micro-organisms, the genes they contain, and the intricate ecosystems they help build into the living environment. Biological diversity is the end result of four billion years of evolution... Estimates of the global number of species range from five million to thirty million. Of these, only 1.4 million species have been given names. The unknown diversity of the world is an unexplored frontier... According to some sources, 15 - 20% of all species on earth may disappear by the year 2000 if human consumption and destruction patterns don't change. This is an extinction rate 1000 times greater than the natural rate.

The Importance of Biological Diversity. A Statement by WWF - World Wide Fund For Nature. pp. 3,4.

35. Gott Peak

Attractions: Views, views, views! **Cautions**: Exposed in poor weather. **Access**: From Blowdown Pass. **Season:** Early June to September. **Rating**: Moderate. **Distance and time:** Straight up from the pass, 2 km (1.3 mi), 2 - 3 hours round trip; via the ridge, 4 km (2.5 mi), 3 - 5 hours round trip. **Elevation gain**: 360 m (1200 ft). **Map**: 92 J/8.

An obvious destination for anyone visiting this area is Gott Peak. On a clear day the views are incomparable. Two basic routes are possible to gain Gott itself: 1) From the pass, ascend directly north and then northwest up a broad open slope to the first summit at 2450 m (8050 ft). From here drop into the dip between the two peaks and scramble up the southeast ridge of 2545 m Gott Peak, with fine views all the way. 2) For an enjoyable half-day trip that gives you more views of the intriguing main Cottonwood Valley, proceed over the pass and along the road for approximately 1.5 km east to a point below the ridge where a discernable saddle (dip) 60 m (200 ft) above is evident - it is easily distinguished on the 1:50,000 map.

A quick scramble up these marmot-mad meadows brings you to the ridge top and fabulous views of the Cottonwood. This can be the starting point for trips to the "Three Summits," "Marmot Gardens," and Gott Peak. To attain Gott, proceed in a westerly direction, erring on the south side of the barren, open ridge. You soon come to a ridge where to continue means cutting across the slopes in a westerly direction. Continue gaining elevation towards your immediate target - the peak directly west of you, 360 m (1200 ft) above the saddle. Once at this unnamed peak, Gott Peak is easily gained by descending to the dip between the two peaks and scrambling up Gott's southeast slopes. Descend via the meadow-covered southwest slopes.

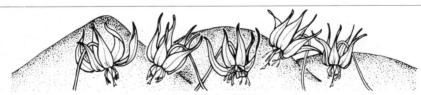

Avalanche lilies

One of the Stein's most colourful alpine floral displays is found on Gott Peak's southern slopes. Soon after snow melt, usually mid to late June, a sea of yellow encompasses these slopes as the early blooming avalanche lilies lead the way of the alpine flowers. Besides providing colour to the alpine, avalanche lilies are also an important food source for grizzly bears. In any remote avalanche path or slope that is home to avalanche lilies and sweetvetch, to name but two, you may find a grizzly digging up the roots of the flowers, which are an essential carbohydrate source for these bruins of the higher country.

36. "Three Summits"

Attractions: Relatively easy access; good views of the Cottonwood Basin. **Cautions:** Carry water; exposed in poor weather; cornices on north side of ridge. **Access**: From Blowdown Pass. **Season**: Late June through September **Distance, time, and elevation gain**: Summit 1: Moderate hike. 5.3 km (3.3 mi); 2 - 3 hours; 240 m (800 ft). Summit 2: Moderate hike. 6.0 km (3.8 mi); 2 hours 30 minutes - 3 hours 15 minutes; 300 m (1000 ft). Summit 3: Strenuous round trip. 14.8 km (9.2 mi). 480 m (1600 ft). **Map**: 92 J/8.

Avalanche lily
(Erythronium grandiflorum) (B.C. Parks)

This high ridge gives closer views of the Cotttonwood area of the Stein that can be obtained from other trips in this section. You do not have to hike all the way to "Summit 3," and in fact the full trip may be too strenuous in hot weather for many day hikers. Backpackers may aim for a small lake south of Summit 3 and use it as a camping base for more leisurely explorations. Fill your water bottles before ascending.

From Blowdown Pass move eastward down the road for 1.5 km (1.0 mi) and then sidehill northeastward to the distinct saddle which lies above the road at 2100 m (7000 ft). This landmark is obvious on the 1:50,000 map. Take special note of the cornices along the ridge. Moving eastward, the ridge is very broad at first, but it narrows above steep scree slopes. Ascend "Summit 1" directly; do not sidehill to the south. The walk to "Summit 2" takes about a half hour. Glimpses of the South Fork of the Cottonwood and of the road can be obtained from rocky outcrops. (The hanging valley to the northwest is "Marmot Gardens," trip # 37.) The view to the south and east is dominated by the mountains on the Stein/Mehatl and Stein/ Kwoiek divides. In the distance to the east is Mount Lytton and the lower canyon.

The ascent of "Summit 3" presents no technical difficulty but means a loss 120 m (400 ft) in elevation, followed by an ascent of 180 m (600 ft). Because of a lingering snow patch on the steep slope to the northeast, you should make the first 90 m (300 ft) of descent to the southeast; then head north and northeast to "Summit 3." For most people, "Summit 3" will be the turnabout point. Only experienced mountaineers should continue, for ahead lies a narrow ridge of unstable, rotten rock. To camp by the small pond at 1995 m (6650 ft) you must descend 180 m (600 ft) from the ridge between "Summits 2 and 3." Do not attempt to descend to the road from this pond; there are cliffs and dangerous slopes below.

Looking southeast from Blowdown Pass (J.R.)

37. "Marmot Gardens"

Attractions: Numerous exploration opportunities; accessible, but rarely visited. **Cautions**: Rough terrain in places; careful of cornices on ridge at start of trip; bear country - exercise caution. **Access**: The ridge west of "Summit 1" (see above description). **Season**: Mid June to late September. **Rating**: Difficult day trip, moderate overnight backpack. **Distance and time**: 8.0 km (5.0 mi); 4 - 5 hours one way, full day return. **Elevation gain**: To ridge, 120 m (400 ft); to "Marmot Gardens" 400 m (1300 ft) **Map**: 92 J/8.

"Marmot Gardens," a large hanging valley, lies north of "Summit 1" and is accessed via the north Cottonwood Creek valley. Your starting point is the ridge just west of "Summit 1" (see trip # 36), where the scree slope is less steep (on the 1:50,000 map these slopes' contour lines are distinctly further apart than the rest of this ridge's north slopes). Proceed to descend in a northeast and then northerly direction down the slope. "Marmot Gardens" is now due north of your present position and is attained by crossing the valley and ascending to the lower meadows.

38. Blowdown Pass to Cottonwood Junction

Attractions: Fine panoramas; accessible alpine; the enchanting North and South Cotton-wood Creeks. **Cautions**: Snow storms not uncommon in the alpine in the summer months; wet forest sections. **Access**: From Blowdown Pass. **Season**: Mid June to late September. **Rating**: Easy - moderate. **Distance and time**: To Silver Queen turnoff, 5.4 km (3.3 mi), 1 hour 30 minutes - 2 hours; to Junction: 13.5 km (8.4 mile), 4 hours. **Elevation change**: Descent of 1170 m (3900 ft) **Maps**: 92 J/8 & 92 I/5.

From Blowdown Pass many different areas of the Stein can be accessed. This route follows the mining exploration road into the South Fork of Cottonwood Creek and ultimately to the junction of the Cottonwood branches. You will descend from the pass at 2145 m (7150 ft) to 1460 m (4800 ft) at the mine turnoff. Take this route when accessing the Silver Queen Mine area. Route-finding is not a concern since the road is clearly visible. Just below the pass on the east side are vast meadows with fine camping in the southwest corner close to the base of the ridge to the west. Continuing along, in dry conditions a shorter route can be gained by dropping from the road you are on to the old road which cuts across the meadows, intersecting the more recently constructed road 2.8 km (1.8 mile) further down.

From the pass, follow the road which lies on the hillside above the forementioned meadows. Past here the road begins to curve and switchback. Roughly 0.3 km (0.2 mi) below the intersection between the old and new roads, a creek crosses the road. The adjacent meadows here offer many fine camping spots. You are now 3.2 km (2.0 mi) from the pass and at an elevation of 1860 m (6200 ft).

The Pika

The pika is a model of cold weather adaptation. Living in the cold subalpine and alpine weather, this relative of the hare and rabbit (thus, the nickname, "rock rabbit") has a small body (averaging 15 cm in length), round ears, and short legs and tail. This body configuration serves to minimize heat loss by exposing the least amount of surface to the cold. Also, a thick fur insulates the pika from head to toe including the inside of the ears and the bottom of the feet so that frost and sharp rocks are not a problem. Plus, the pika's body temperature is 2 - 3° C higher than other small mammals. As a result, this cold winter body is so efficient that it cannot withstand temperatures above 28° C for more than a couple of hours. Hence, on hot summer days you will find pikas inside their cool rock dwellings, escaping the heat outside.

Tiger lily
(Lilium columbianum)
A 20 - 70 cm tail, orange flowered plant found from valley bottom to subalpine. (N.B.)

The remainder of the road to the mine turnoff is punctuated with meadows above and below the road, avalanche paths, and fine views. Several streams cross the road making for wet travel in the early summer. 8.6 km (5.4 mi), 1 - 2 hours, from the pass is a bridge that crosses the Cottonwood, leading to the Silver Queen Mine diggings. Rough camping sites are situated on the north side of the creek. To continue to Silver Queen Mine, see trip # 39.

0.5 km (0.3 mi) east of the Silver Queen Mine turnoff, the road descends to the creek and proceeds up the south side. At this point look for a well-marked and cleared trail. The going is slower as you move through flowered meadows and bush. The remainder of the distance to the junction is straightforward as you follow the trail above the creek, never varying more than a few hundred metres distance from it. The descent is gradual until reaching the slopes above the confluence of the north and south forks of Cottonwood Creek, where you descend about 120 m (400 ft), passing an old trapper's cabin only 0.3 km (0.2 mi) from the creek crossing. Once on the banks of the main creek move downstream approximately 100 m to the crossing - a large log with a rope railing. A beautifully situated camp with a food cache, fire circle, and rough tent sites is found here, elevation 1065 m (3550 ft). Check out the spruce here - there are some big ones. To continue the trek to the Stein River and Cottonwood Creek camp see trip # 41.

39. South Cottonwood Creek to Silver Queen Mine

Attractions: Open, parkland covered ridges; excellent views of the Stein. **Cautions**: Carry water when climbing in this dry area. **Access:** From the South Fork of Cottonwood Creek, 5.4 km (3.3 mi) east of Blowdown Pass on the mining exploration road. **Season**: Late June - September. **Rating**: Moderate. **Distance and time**: 5.5 km (3.4 mi); 1 hour 30 minutes - 2 hours 30 minutes to the upperlake. **Elevation gain**: To the upper lake, 390 m (1300 ft). **Map**: 92 J/8.

For a great ridge walk and access to the tiring but rewarding "Angel's Walk" (see trip # 40), take this route. While the road has damaged the area considerably, it does provide relatively easy access to the alpine.A well constructed bridge crosses the Cottonwood at the point where you leave the road - fill your water bottles here. The road soon switchbacks. After the third switchback a road which accesses diggings on the west side of the mine area intersects on the right. Continue straight ahead.

A steady climb for another 20 - 45 minutes brings you to a basin at 1770 m (5900 ft) in which resides a boarded up mine shaft, mine tailings, etc. - all the ugly stuff of an old mine.

To continue to the uppermost lake, proceed along the road you were travelling following as it curves around to the east, passing mining debris, and switchbacks three times. Just past the first switchback, a road intersects from the left followed by a levelling off of the road and another road on your left. Past this road only 200 - 300 m are several more roads intersecting the main road. You should be able to see a lake with several adjacent buildings down below and to the east.

Continuing forward, proceed to a basin with a meadow-strewn ridge forming a backdrop and a lake in the basin's western half. A forest is on the northern fringes of the basin. The road continues to the uppermost workings in the southeast corner of the basin. Small caves are visible above the road's terminus. You are now at an enchanting spot which makes an excellent base camp for exploring this area. On the northwest corner of the basin, just into the woods, is a suitable camping site. In drier months, fine camping is found on a small flat meadow, 45 m (150 ft) above the road's terminus. See the next trip description (# 40) to continue beyond here.

> *"I hope and pray that this area will be reserved...for people who will treat it gently and share it with others. A hundred years from now I can imagine a doctor pre-scribing a trip through the Stein for one who needs to regain a basic rhythm of life and a faith in human nature too. The Stein Valley would be a living testimony to the truth that one generation of this province considered the needs of the next. They would find to their joy one resource of our province that cannot be renewed or restored - the beauty of this land as it came from the hand of God."*
>
> Father Damasus

Golden eagle
(Aquila chrysaetos)
A resident of high mountain ridges and open tundra, the large golden eagle (wingspan up to 2 m) can be seen soaring over its range without rest for several hours. Favourite snacks: Marmots, snowshoe hares, ptarmigan, jays, and crows. Look for these majestic birds gliding over the meadows near Blowdown Pass. (L.V.E.C.)

40. Silver Queen Mine to Stein River

Attractions: Fabulous views of North Scudamore, main Stein. **Cautions**: Steep slopes with loose footing and abundant wind-fall; carry lots of water - fill up at the upper lake; exposed in poor weather. **Access**: From upper lake in Silver Queen Mine area (see previous description). **Season**: Mid June to late September. **Rating**: Difficult. **Distance and time**: 10.6 km (6.6 mi), full day. **Season**: Mid-June - September. **Elevation change**: Descent of 1450 m (4800 ft) **Maps**: 92 J/8 and 92 I/5.

Varied thrush
(*Exoreus naevius*)
Similar in size, shape, and appearance to the robin. Distinguished by its orange coloured breast, which has a dark band across it, and an orange eye-stripe with orange bars on the wing. Found primarily in forests, especially on the forest floor where it searches for insects, worms, fruits, and seeds. (R.B.C.M.)

Appropriately titled the "Angel's Walk" (angels with muscular thighs and healthy knees, no doubt) by the late Father Damasus, a contributor to *Exploring the Stein River Valley*, this is one of the more scenic routes in the entire watershed. It is also demanding; do not travel this knee-burner unless you are experienced in route-finding. Starting at the highest lake in the Silver Queen Mine area (see the end of trip # 39), proceed to the southeast corner of the basin you are in and ascend the slopes near the end of the road in a southeast direction. A flat area is quickly reached - a fine camping spot once the ground has dried from the winter snowpack. Continue in a southeast direction up the next slopes, which give way to a southwest-northeast lying ridge offering great views of Stein and Siwhe Mountains to the east, the "Three Summits" and Gott Peak to the northwest.

You must now move in a southwest direction up the ridge to the 2130 m (7150 ft) peak south of the lake. The route along this ridge top is easily followed and has good footing. Approximately 1 hour from the lake, you are now on top of the peak. Views of the North Scudamore and south ridge of the Stein are gained from here. For those making a day-trip from Blowdown Pass, this may be your destination. If based near the uppermost lake, you may want to ramble westward along the open ridge top. Be sure to take note of the terrain here - it is classic parkland landscape that is found on warm, dry, and steep southern slopes; whitebark pine and subalpine fir trees predominate interspersed with meadow, heath, and grassland.

To begin the "Angel's Walk" proper, move due south and then east along the distinct ridge top. Your first destination is the small summit east-southeast of the 2130 m (7150 ft) starting point, roughly 1 km distant. Overall, err on the south side of this ridge. 45 minutes - 1 hour travel from the 2130 m (7150 ft) peak, this small peak, elevation 2100 m (7000 ft), is the meeting point of several ridges. Continuing along, move directly east into the small dip west of the next small peak, losing 60 m (200 ft), and then southeast along the ridge top to a small, distinctly round topped summit, elevation 2010 m (6700 ft). Views of the main Stein valley become more frequent now.

Once atop this small rounded peak the route should be obvious as you want to continue in a southeast direction to the next peak at 1980 m (6600 ft). The easiest route is to stay close to the east side of the ridge top since it is more open and has rough game trails. Atop this broad ridge, you are at an important junction. The ridge splits here with one arm extending southwest towards the Scudamore basin, another in a northeast direction into Cottonwood Canyon, and the other (the one you want to take) dropping in a southeast direction towards Cotton-wood Creek and the Stein.

From the 1980 m (6600 ft) peak, descend in a easterly direction about 0.5 km to where the southeast tending ridge is apparent and then proceed in a southeast direction along this ridge. Now the route-finding becomes more difficult as you enter into the western pine, subalpine fir, and Engelmann spruce forest. Continuing in a southeast direction (Kent Lake and Creek, which lie between Petlushkwohap and Skihist Mountains to the south, are your best reference point), stay on the west side of the vegetated slopes up to the ridge top (which is apparent with the drops to east and west). Eventually the ridge flattens out before continuing a gradual descent and then climb of 5 - 10 minutes to the final peak at an elevation of 1680 m (5600 ft).

Now move along the eastward-pointing ridge (well-defined on the map), dropping about 300 m (1000 ft) to the 1350 m (4500 ft) contour. From here move in a southeast direction, being sure to avoid moving easterly into the Cottonwood Canyon. Prolific windfall and loose footing make for slow travel in the final 690 m (2300 ft) of descent. Use Kent Falls as a reference point when moving down the tree-covered slopes. Eventually you will come out near Cottonwood Creek with the main Stein trail no more than 10 minutes away. Follow the orange markers to the crossing downstream to reach Cotton-wood camp, situated on the east side of Cottonwood Creek.

41. Cottonwood Junction to Stein River

Attractions: Great views of the Stein from just above Cotton-wood Camp; the quickest and easiest way to connect the Stein River and alpine regions. **Cautions**: Loose footing on the slopes above Cottonwood Creek camp; questionable water from Cattle Valley Creek. **Access**: From Blowdown Pass, 13.5 km along the road and trail (see trip # 38). **Season**: Early June - October. **Rating**: Moderate. **Distance and time**: 8.5 km (5.3 mi); 4 - 6 hours. **Elevation change**: Descent of 390 m (1300 ft). **Map**: 92 I/5.

Leaving the upper Cottonwood, you hike towards the Cot-tonwood's lower canyon while travelling along a well con-

Fireweed
(Epilobium angustifolium)
Found from valley bottom to subalpine, especially in old burns and clearings. Easily identified by its height (up to 1.5 m), pink-purple flowers, and tall, slender profile. Native people harvested the vitamin C rich shoots of fireweed. (B.C. Parks)

structed trail. The views are limited on the northern three quarters of the hike, but are quite spectacular on the southern end above the Cottonwood Canyon and the Stein.

The first 4.5 km (2.8 mi) is straight-forward as the well marked and cleared trail rolls along the east side of the Cottonwood, never more than 90 m (300 ft) above the river. Several small sidecreeks make for muddy sections in places. 1 hour 30 minutes - 2 hours travel brings you to Cattle Valley Creek, elevation about 990 m (3300 ft). A rough camp

Divorce is out of the Question

Everybody knows the old adage about it being hard to see the forest for the trees. In the Stein River Valley, it can sometimes be hard to see the trees for the lichens.

Check this for yourself by pausing a moment along the trail. If you've chosen your stopping place well, and if you look closely, you'll see that what you had always assumed were just tree trunks and tree branches are also actually patchwork quilts of living lichens. On some trees you may have a hard time finding bark that isn't covered by lichens of a dozen or more kinds.

The same is true of the Stein's boulders and rocky outcroppings. These are not the cold, inanimate things they may at first seem; their surfaces are very much alive with lichens of every imaginable hue and texture. Isn't it time you slowed down to take a closer look?

The first thing to know about lichens (pronounced "LIKE-ens") is that they are fungi. There are approximately 100,000 different fungi, most of which are microscopic. Of those large enough to be seen by the naked eye, some familiar ones include the meadow mushroom, the morrel, and the bread mould.

Unlike flowering plants, but like most animals, fungi don't produce their own carbohydrates; to survive they must "eat."

Some fungi eat decaying matter. Others eat plants. Others again eat animals - even living people. Loosely defined, a lichen is a fungus that eats algae. Though some kinds of algae, including seaweed, can be large, the ones that lichen fungi associate with are very small. So small, in fact, that they live inside the weft of fungal threads that is the lichen.

Most fungi live hidden away inside the hosts they feed on. You'll see them, if at all, only during the few weeks of the year when they develop fruiting bodies such as mushrooms. Because lichen fungi, however, actually envelop their food host, they themselves are able to grow exposed to view. Think of lichens as living fungal greenhouses wherein algae simultaneously grow and provide food for the host fungi. In essence, both of the "partners" benefit: The lichen fungus has a reliable food source and the algae gains a home.

Not that lichens necessarily look much like greenhouses - though at times they seem to resemble just about everything else. In general, however, it is convenient to distinguish seven different groupings, namely the dust lichens, the crust lichens, the scale lichens, the leaf lichens, the club lichens, the shrub lichens, and the hair lichens. A little careful

with a fire circle, food rope, and space for a couple of tents is on the creek's north side. Crossing the creek's channels on fallen logs 100 m upstream from camp - look for the orange markers. You are now 3.6 km (2.2 mi) from Cottonwood Creek camp.

The trail now ascends above the steep canyon walls further downstream. Numerous steep switchbacks made slower by loose footing take you out of the Cattle Valley Creek depression and up to gentler terrain at roughly 1080 m (3600 ft) A well-established trail

lichen-looking along the trails of the Stein should turn up all of these.

In the valley bottom, you won't have to look far to find the Wolf Lichen (*Letharia vulpina*) - a little, shrubby, sunshine-coloured thing very common over Douglas-fir and Ponderosa pine. The Wolf Lichen contains vulpinic acid, and is mildly poisonous. In Scandinavia, it was once mixed with ground glass, and sprinkled over wolf bait - apparently to good effect. Hence the name. Closer to home, the Thompson Indians are said to have used this species as a body and face paint, and as a dye for their animal skins. A colourful species no matter how you cut it.

Underfoot, watch for the Freckle Lichen (*Peltigera apththosa*), one of the largest of all leaf lichens. Just look for what resemble emerald green (turquoise when dry) scatter rugs laid out here and there over the forest floor. Peppered over their upper surface are numerous tiny "freckles" - technically "cephalodia." These are actually tiny colonies of nitrogen-fixing cyanobacteria; for here is a lichen that is made up of not two, but three different organisms. What is more, each of these derives from a separate kingdom of life. The only kingdoms not represented in the Freckle Lichen are the Animal Kingdom and the Protista.

As you climb higher, the branches of the trees become heavily laden with hair lichens. These belong mostly to the genus *Bryoria*, and come in many different species. To tell them apart, notice their different colours, their different sizes, and their "dandruff," or "soredia." (Some will have it, while others won't.) Farther north, these same hair lichens are the main winter food of the mountain caribou. In earlier times, they also provided a winter staple for the native peoples who gathered them (especially *Bryoria fremontii*) to steam with berries as a kind of vegetarian Salish pemmican. An acquired taste, you can be sure.

Trevor Goward

sidehills above the Cottonwood Canyon for the next 1.1 km (0.7 mi). Since leaving Cattle Valley Creek you have either climbed or been on the level above the canyon. Look for a small pond on the east side of the trail below a small rock face where you begin to descend to the Stein 360 m (1200 ft) below.

0.6 km (0.4 mi) past the pond, you descend into a small basin and climb up the south side, at the top of which is a flat rock outcrop, "Unnecessary Knob," elevation approximately 780 m (2600 ft). Keep parallel to the canyon at first and then move in a southeast direction. As you come onto the top of a rough and steep rocky section look for cairns and orange tape and slowly descend down the slopes. Once below the steepest slopes aim for a large fir tree in the middle of a boulder field and then angle towards the Cottonwood Canyon. Kent Falls should be visible across the valley.

You must now switchback down the slopes, encountering more boulders and varying degrees of steepness. The dry open forest becomes thicker and the trail flattens out as you descend the last 0.4 km (0.3 mi) to the junction with the main Stein trail. Look for a sign indicating "Stein Lake 30 km, Blowdown Pass 20 km". Cottonwood camp is only 100 m away, situated on the creek's east side. Cottonwood Falls, one of the focal points of the valley and a refreshing stop on hot days, is only 10 minutes travel upstream from the camp on the Cottonwood's east bank.

Cottonwood Falls (N.B.)

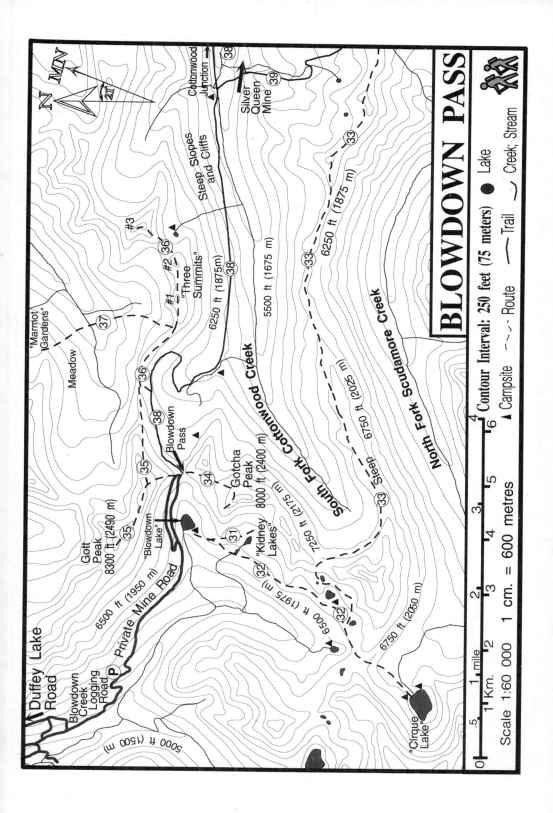

BLOWDOWN PASS

Contour Interval: 250 feet (75 meters) ● Lake
▲ Campsite   -·- Route   — Trail   ~ Creek; Stream

Scale 1:60 000   1 cm. = 600 metres

Duffey Lake Road
Blowdown Creek Logging Road
5000 ft (1500 m)
Private Mine Road
6500 ft (1950 m)
Gott Peak 8300 ft (2490 m)
"Blowdown Lake"
Blowdown Pass
Gotcha Peak 8000 ft (2400 m)
"Kidney Lakes"
7250 ft (2175 m)
6500 ft (1975 m)
6750 ft (2050 m)
"Cirque Lake"
"Marmot Gardens"
Meadow
"Three Summits"
#1 #2 #3
Steep Slopes and Cliffs
6250 ft (1875m)
5500 ft (1675 m)
South Fork Cottonwood Creek
North Fork Scudamore Creek
6250 ft (1875 m)
6750 ft (2025 m)
Steep
Cottonwood Junction
Silver Queen Mine

N   MN
21°

NORTH STEIN

The North Stein is best described in one word: Wild. Be prepared for a bushy entrance and exit, unbelievable numbers of mosquitoes, rough terrain, and volatile weather. This is bear country - be sure to make your presence known.

Ecological overview: The majority of the terrain covered in the following route descriptions are in the alpine tundra zone. The North Stein's high snowfalls are conducive to heather meadows, which are characterized by evergreen dwarf shrubs, rowberry, blueberries, and heathers. The lower reaches of the North Stein include coastal forest species such as Pacific silver fir, western hemlock, huckleberries, white rhododendron, and false azalea.

42. Van Horlick Road to Van Horlick Pass

Attractions: Flowered meadows; isolation. **Cautions:** Cold, wet weather; bear country. **Access:** From terminus of east fork of Van Horlick Creek Logging Road. **Season:** Mid-June to October. **Rating:** Moderate. **Distance and time:** About 2 km (1.3 mi); Return day trip (bushwhack) to pass. **Elevation gain:** 285 m (950 ft).**Map:** 92 J/8.

While a short route to the Stein's alpine, this trip involves at least an hour of bush-whacking and is wet in the lower section near the creek. From the road end, head south down through thick woods to the creek and then follow the creek. After approximately 1.0 km (0.6 mi), move in a southeast direction. The bush eventually gives way to rocky terrain. Large meadows greet you at the pass, elevation 1875 m (6250 ft). Numerous camping sites can be found on the Stein side of the pass. The ridge to the northeast may be ascended without technical difficulty to the summit at 2250 m (7500 ft). Be prepared for cold, wet weather in this area.

Spring beauty

(*Claytonia lanceolata*)
An easily recognized 10 - 20 cm tall flower with two broad leaves and white or pale-pink flowers. Found from valley bottom to alpine in meadows and open woods. Blooms in early spring at lower elevations, mid-summer in the alpine. (B. C. Parks)

43. North Stein Viewpoint

Attractions: Views that no camera can bring back. **Cautions:** Rough, exposed terrain. **Access:** From Van Horlick Pass. **Season:** Mid-July through September. **Rating:** Easy - moderate. **Distance and time:** 1.6 km (1.0 mi) one way; 5.6 km (3.5 mi) round trip via meadows; 30 minutes, one way; 2 hours round trip via meadows. **Elevation gain:** 300 m (1000 ft), 490 m (1600 ft) via meadows. **Map:** 92 J/8.

What a Beauty

The corms of this plant were formerly an important "root" food for the Nlaka' pamux... They were usually dug from late May to late June, during or immediately after flowering: at this time the corms could be easily located. One could also dig them later in the summer or fall if he knew where to dig. Ranging from pea-sized to golfball-sized, the corms are usually found from 4 - 8 cm below the surface. The older the plant, the larger its corm... Formerly they were cooked in under-ground pits, like avalanche lily corms, or steamed in watertight baskets using red-hot rocks... The corms could also be dried immediately after they were dug. They were often cooked, then mashed and formed into little loaves, about 3 - 4 cm thick, then dried on mats.

Turner, Nancy et al, *Thompson Ethnobotany*, Royal B.C. Museum. 1990, p. 240.

From the meadows on the south side of the pass proceed south towards a distinct summit. You may find it easiest to follow a small creek upstream in a southwest direction to its source at a small tarn not shown on the 1:50,000 topographic map. The rounded summit is easily gained, rewarding you with excellent views of the North Stein.

44. North Stein Meadows

Attractions: Abundant flora and fauna, especially flowers in early summer. **Cautions:** Bear country. **Access:** From Van Horlick Pass. **Season:** Mid-July to September. **Rating:** Moderate. **Distance and time:** 4.3 km (2.7 mi) round trip; 4 - 5 hours round trip. **Elevation gain:** On return to pass 210 m (700 ft). **Map:** 92 J/8.

From Van Horlick Pass descend southeasterly about 100 m (350 ft) to the extremely flat upper meadow. The only other prominent feature here is a canal-like stream whose banks, unlike the lush enclosing valley sides, support few flowers because of their poor drainage and lingering snow. The stream and its banks provide home and food for various small mammals.

As the creek begins to cascade to the lower meadow, the vegetation changes from short sedges to chest-high hellebore. In the distance the peaks around Stein Lake are evident. There are large displays of Indian paintbrush (both red and white), and mimulus along the mossy banks. A small pond is home to numerous frogs.

The meadows end where the valley drops steeply to the North Stein 300 m (1000 ft) below. From here you can see the effects of avalanches that have swept down the east ridge and dislodged trees on the opposite side of the valley.

45. North Stein Ridge from Van Horlick Pass

Mountain chickadee
(Parus gambeli)
From June to September, this chickadee frequents the semi-open coniferous forests of the subalpine. Distinguish it from the similar black-capped chickadee by noting whether the cap is solid black; if the cap is broken by a white eye-line, then it is a mountain chickadee. (R.B.C.M.)

Attractions: Spectacular views; wildlife. **Cautions:** Carry water; volatile weather; exposed terrain. **Access:** From Van Horlick Pass, 1905 m (6250 ft). **Season:** Mid-July to September. **Rating:** Moderate - difficult. **Distance and time:** 12.8 km (8.0 mi) round trip; Full day round trip. **Elevation gain:** 510 m (1700 ft) or 750 m (2500 ft) depending upon the route chosen. **Map:** 92 J/8.

From the pass, ascend the steep trail northeast to the knob at 2060 m (6750 ft). Now you have a choice: Less energetic hikers can sidehill east-southeast to the 2025 m (6750 ft) saddle; others may wish to make the steep climb to the 2265 m (7550 ft) ridge above. Once on the ridge, head southeast over huge granite blocks to the main summit. The panorama from here includes a vertical silver thread that is Elton Lake Falls.

From the saddle, continue southeast to a second, gentler 2250 m (7600 ft) summit. The third summit to the south may be avoided by sidehilling along flowered slopes at the 2190 m (7300 ft) level on the west. Descend into another broad saddle at 2175 m (7250 ft), where snow-melt to the east should provide water. Mountaineering routes begin here. You may return to the pass by reversing your approach, but a good alternative is to descend 150 m (500 ft) before contouring northwest along a shoulder through meadows at the 1980 m (6600 ft) level. This traverse below the steep cliffs and scree slopes leads back towards Van Horlick Pass. Because of the steepness of the slopes, avoid descending directly to the meadows visible below.

Looking south from the North Stein Ridge (R.S.)

46. Van Horlick/Scudamore Divide

Attractions: The rarely visited Scudamore basin; wildlife; spectacular views. **Cautions:** Exposed; rough terrain; route finding skills are essential. **Access:** From Van Horlick Pass, 1905 m (6250 ft). **Season:** Mid-July to September. **Rating:** Moderate - difficult. **Distance and time:** 16 km (10.0 mi), full day. **Elevation gain:** 275 m (900 ft) to Scudamore meadows; 610 m (2000 ft) for full descent. **Map:** 92 J/8.

From Van Horlick Pass descend a short distance north to cross a boulder field, then ascend northeast to the bottom of a large meadow. Cross the creek and meadow and pass into an open basin punctuated with large boulders approximately 2.4 km (1.5 mi) from the pass. A shallow tarn (not shown on the 1:50,000 map) at 2040 m (6800 ft) gives wonderful reflections of the mountains to the west. Ascend 60 m (200 ft) east to the divide between Van Horlick Creek, which you are in, and Scudamore Creek (Stein divide). On the Scudamore side there is good camping, and water is available from snow-melt.

Two or more routes are possible from here. A high route, which provides outstanding views, climbs north from the divide, following the ridge-top to a high point at 2205 m (7350 ft). A lower, more sheltered route (sometimes snow-bound until August) leads through the meadows east of the ridge at about the 2100 m (7000-ft) level, passing a small tarn at 2100 m. A few hundred paces farther north is a second tarn set in a deep hollow. Descend to this tarn (which has no outflow) and climb the shoulder on the north side to join the high route on the ridge above. This ridge then dips gently to 2145 m (7150 ft) before ascending the final bump that offers a fine panorama for a lunch spot.

Hikers camped in the North Stein may wish to return from here; it is feasible to descend 150 m (500 ft) into the pass to the northeast and then sidehill to three small lakes at about 2175 m (7250 ft). The lakeside has room for two or three tents, but is exposed. The broad ridge above may be hiked in either direction. A return via the ridge, rather than across the meadows, will probably be the quickest.

Grey wolf
(Canis lupis)
Rarely seen, but occasionally heard, the wolf is certainly one of the most striking symbols of wilderness. (N.W.P.S.)

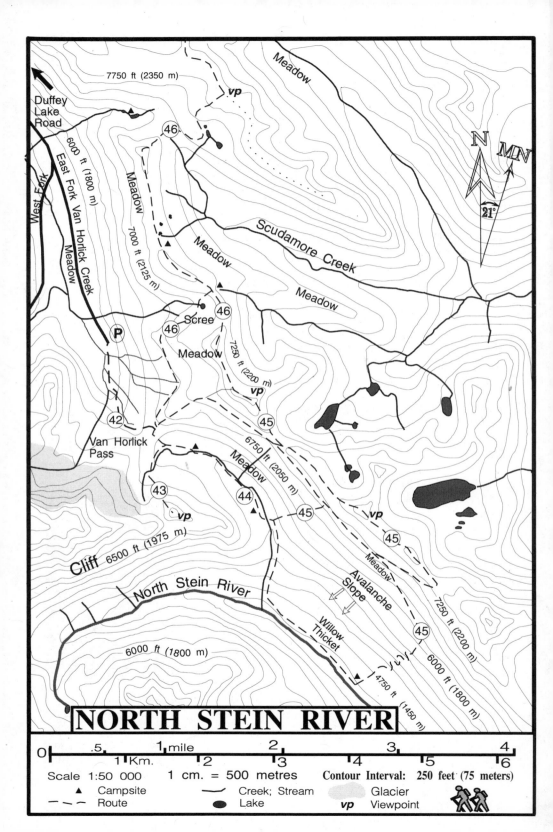

NORTH STEIN RIVER

Scale 1:50 000   1 cm. = 500 metres   Contour Interval: 250 feet (75 meters)

▲ Campsite   — Creek; Stream   ░ Glacier
– – – Route   ● Lake   vp Viewpoint

The Scudamore Creek drainage in winter (N.B.)

KAYAKING THE STEIN

A sad reflection of the destruction of B.C.'s forests and rivers is the fact that the Stein is one of the very few rivers left in southern B.C. that is still in a wilderness state. Having witnessed the powerful rapids of this untamed river's lower canyon, most people are content to enjoy the river from the safe and dry river banks. Exploration of these waters is a challenge that even the most skilled and experienced whitewater paddlers rarely consider. Unless you are accustomed to paddling grade V+ water do not even entertain any notions of paddling the Stein.

At the time of printing, the Stein had been run in its entirety only once. Eric Ridington, Robin Barley, and Ian Taylor made the descent over the Labour Day weekend, 1989. Prior to this, Klaus Streckman had paddled the central portion of the river and a number of people had run the four km section between the Stein trail parking lot and the Fraser.

The river can be divided roughly into three sections: The upper canyon, the middle Stein, and the lower canyon. The difficult whitewater is concentrated in the upper and lower canyons, with the central portion being relatively calm. What follows is a general description of these three sections. Those wanting a more detailed description should refer to Eric Ridington's article "First Descent of the Stein River," published in the October 20, 1989 issue of The Paddle Post, which is available through Sport B.C.

The Upper Canyon

Access to the upper canyon is by float plane via Stein Lake or by helicopter. Gravel bars near the confluence of Rutledge Creek with the Stein are the best launching points. The upper canyon is the most remote part of the trip - if you have problems you're on your own!

From Stein Lake to the beginning of the upper canyon is approximately nine km, the first few km of which is obstructed by logs and other hazards. The remainder is class II with several sections of challenging rapids (III-IV). Once at the canyon the fun begins. Extending for about eight km and dropping as much as 120 m per km (400 ft per mile) in some sections, the upper canyon becomes more continuous, but less severe as it progresses. There are over 24 distinct drops in this section of the river, along with six class V rapids and two as yet unattempted class VI waterfalls. Scouting is crucial.

The Middle Stein

This section consists of 30 km of relatively easy class II. The attractions of this section include abundant wildlife (deer, bear, beaver and mosquitoe to name but a few) and numerous gravel bar campsites. Just before the cable crossing there is a short section of class III, a convenient warm-up for the rigors of the lower canyon.

The Lower Canyon

Just below the cable crossing the river falls away into 15 km of continuous class IV and V+, dropping 60 - 90 m per km (200 - 300 ft per mile). There are approximately 12 class V rapids and numerous class IV rapids. Two sections worthy of respect are the "Devil's Escalator" and the "Devil's Staircase" sections. The "Devil's Escalator" starts roughly three km downstream from the teepee, a prominent landmark on the south bank of the river. A five m waterfall starts this section followed by 150 m of class V. The "Devil's Staircase," farther downriver, is 150 m of class V+, dropping in a series of one to five m high waterfalls. Both these sections may be portaged without too much difficulty. Once the Trailhead parking lot is reached, a four km section of class III - IV+ paddling remains before exiting into the Fraser River.

It is possible to carry your boats to the cable crossing and put in there, thus allowing for shorter and more accessible paddling. Mid - August to mid - September, after the runoff, is the safest time to paddle the Stein. At high water the river more than doubles its volume, making paddling considerably more dangerous. It must be stressed that even at low water, the Stein is only for advanced, well prepared kayakers.

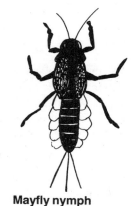

Mayfly nymph
(naiad) (order Emphemeroptera)
Found in fast-flowing rocky streams. This 1.5 cm long insect has a green, brown, and transparent body with slim legs and three filaments on the end. It is smaller than the similar damselfly and stonefly larvae. (B.C. Parks)

Running the upper canyon (R.B.)

WINTER RECREATION

Ski-touring

As the winter snowfalls begin to accumulate in December, the Stein transforms into a ski-touring paradise. A seemingly endless array of terrain and abundant dry snow make this relatively unexplored area worth visiting. The following is a brief overview of the more easily accessed skiing areas within and adjacent to the Stein. None of the described areas can be accessed without at least five hours of travel, however.

Note: Ski-touring requires special equipment, skills, and knowledge. Avalanche safety, proper equipment, and intermediate skiing ability are requisites for all persons intending to visit the Stein's slopes in the winter. In other words, this section is only for experienced backcountry skiers.

Texas Creek

From Texas Creek's East Fork, access is gained to the alpine areas surrounding "Brimful Lake" and the Siwhe Creek - Cattle Valley divide. The relatively low snowfall of the Lillooet area will normally allow you to drive at least part way up Texas Creek. Proceed to the final junction of the East Fork, 22.3 km (14.0 mi) from the West Side Road (see Road Access section for details). At this junction you can gain the "Brimful Lake" area via the right fork, which crosses the creek and extends for approximately 0.3 km (0.2 mi), or the Siwhe Creek - Cattle Valley divide via the left fork, which also terminates within a few hundred metres. From there, a great variety of skiing can be accessed.

The "Brimful Lake" access route crosses some steep slopes that should be avoided in times of higher avalanche hazard. Proceed to the col to the west, elevation 2085 m (6950 ft), which is clearly identified on the map. Once at the pass, "Brimful Lake" can be gained directly by proceeding southwest and then south until at the small ridge north of Brimful. Alternately, a safer route in higher avalanche conditions is to proceed west and then southwest from the pass for about 1.5 km (1.0 mi), losing roughly 200 m (670 ft) elevation before climbing in a southeast direction to Brimful.

The Siwhe Creek - Cattle Valley access begins by gaining the southwest corner of the cutblock above the road's terminus. A trail should be identifiable at the beginning of the forest. The trail proceeds east through forest for about 0.5 km (0.3 mi) before opening up. To the southeast is a col that provides access to the numerous slopes around "Devils Lake" and Cattle Valley. If the slopes are of questionable stability, use the forested valley southwest of the previous route. Starting at the top of the same cutblock, head southeast, quickly gaining elevation and soon entering a forested valley, which extends up to the col at the south end, elevation 2055 m (6850 ft).

Blowdown Pass - Cottonwood Creek

Access is via Blowdown Creek. The 14 km (8.8 mi), 900 m (3000 ft) ascent from the Duffey Lake Road to "Blowdown Lake" requires at least six hours of steady climbing. Several avalanche tracks from the slopes to the east intersect the road - be sure to assess the conditions. The greatest avalanche danger is found beneath Gott Peak's southwest slopes. If the snowpack is questionable, move south to the open forest and meadows below the road. Cornices are normally quite pronounced on the ridge between Gott Peak and "Summit One" as are the ridge tops between Blowdown Pass and "Cirque Lake."

The Opportunist on the Move

Especially broad-ranging in its perpetual quest for food (its latin name is Gulo gulo, meaning "glutton glutton"), the elusive wolverine will cover a territory of up to (an unbelievably big!) 2000 square km. This fierce and aloof carnivore is highly opportunistic. When it is not able to kill small mammals such as muskrats and beavers, fierce fighters in their own right, the wolverine will sometimes drive even bears and cougars from their kills! In winter, the deep snow slows down bigger animals, allowing the wolverine to hunt mountain goat, deer, and moose.

In ski-touring the Stein's alpine, one is almost assured of seeing wolverine tracks that appear to go forever across the ridge tops. Wolverine tracks are easily identified by their 10 - 18 cm length and five toe marks. If you are fortunate enough to cross tracks with this increasingly rare animal, look for a one metre long, thickly furred, dark brown creature with a broad light stripe along each side and a proportionally small head. Nicknamed "skunk bear" because of its bear like appearance and disagreeable musk, which is used to mark its kills and carrion, the wolverine is one animal that cannot tolerate man's presence. Protection of large wilderness areas is essential if this amazing weasel is to survive.

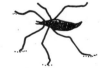

Snow crane fly
(Chionea spp.)
One insect you are almost assured of seeing on the snow is the crane fly. This 5 - 12 mm long wingless insect looks like a spider at first glance, but it has only 6 legs, whereas spiders have 8. (M.M.)

Researching the skiing section of this book was, of course, strictly serious work. (L.d.)

Within this area you will find excellent skiing. Numerous peaks, ridges, and slopes are found in the North Scudamore area, while closer to "Blowdown Lake" there are several summits and slopes worth visiting. East of Blowdown Pass, the southwest-facing slopes below "Summit One" provide for some good tree-skiing. If snow conditions are stable, an ascent of Gott Peak followed by a ski down its southwest slopes is a possibility. On poor weather days the avalanche tracks off the road west of "Blowdown Lake" provide short, steep powder runs.

Van Horlick Creek - Scudamore Creek

The east fork of Van Horlick Creek logging road provides access to relatively unexplored terrain in the North Stein and Scudamore Creek. The access is long and relatively flat since you must ski from Duffey Lake Road to the end of the east fork, 15.3 km (9.5 mi). Elevation gain and time from Duffey Lake Road to the end of the East Fork: 435 m (1450 ft) ; 5 - 7 hours.

The east fork branches off from the mainline, 8.9 km (5.5 mi) from the Duffey Lake Road. At the terminus of the East Fork, elevation 1620 m (5300 ft), Van Horlick Pass, elevation 1875 m (6250 ft), lies only 2.0 km to the south and is easily gained from the road end.

Northeast of the end of the east fork road is another pass that gives access to the headwaters of Scudamore Creek. To reach this pass, ski to the top of the cutblock at the east fork road's end. Pick up a gully in the forest at the south corner of the cutblock and follow it straight up to treeline. Avalanche danger at the top can be avoided in the trees on the north side. From the top of the gully, contour north into an attractive basin offering good campsites. The pass is at the top of the basin and leads over into Scudamore Creek. Good ski slopes abound on both sides of the pass. Total time from east fork terminus to the pass with Scudamore Creek: About 3 hours.

Another access to this same general area lies north of Van Horlick's east fork. About 6.3 km (3.9 mi) along the mainline is a branch road that climbs for approximately 4.0 km (2.5 mi) to 1650 m (5500 ft). The slopes further southwest reportedly offer fine skiing. Further exploration into Scudamore Creek may be possible via the col at 1820 m (6075 ft).

Springtails

On warm winter days in the subalpine and alpine, the shuffle of one's skis may send the "fleas of the snowpack," springtails (order collembola) jumping in every direction. These small (2 - 6 mm long) wingless insects would not be noticed if it were not for their leaping ability. Springtails have an abdominal tail called a furcula which extends forward and is secured and released by a catch mechanism. When the springtail wants to move, its catch mechanism releases the fucula, resulting in a springing action, propelling the springtail 10 - 15 cm into the air. These primitive insects actually spend most of their time on the ground eating pollen, fungus, and leaf debris. Once the adults are mature (November to March), they climb up vegetation and rocks to reach the snow surface, where they mate in swarms covering areas up to several square km in size.

Lizzie Lake

Access to the Lizzie Cabin alpine is gained via the Lillooet Lake and Lizzie Creek roads. In exceptionally cold winters the Lillooet Lake Road may not be passable (contact the Squamish District Forestry office, (604) 898-9671, for road conditions). From the Lizzie Creek - Lillooet Lake junction, you face approximately 15 km (9 mi), 1260 m (4200 ft) of ascent to Lizzie Cabin. Average time: Seven hours. The Lizzie Lake Road presents few avalanche dangers except for the predictable, road-blocking slide from the north slopes approximately 6 km (3.8 mi) from the start. By late April this avalanche has normally melted and the road may be travelled by four-wheel drive to below the first steep switchback, 8 km (5 mi) from Lillooet Lake.

Once at Lizzie Lake, the cabin is most easily reached by crossing the lake to its southeast corner and then ascending through the forest in a east-northeast direction, staying within 100 m (330 ft) of the creek depression to the southeast. You should reach the bench west of the "Gates of Shangri-La," elevation 1560 m (5200 ft). From here, the cabin is easily found by following the creek for approximately 10 - 15 minutes.

Ruffed grouse
(*Bonasa umbellus*)
One of the more frequently seen residents of the Stein's valley bottom is the ruffed grouse. Listen for the male's distinct drumming call during breeding season from March to May. (M.M.)

Like other members of the dog family, the grey wolf's tracks consist of four toes, with toenails normally showing, and a distinct heel pad, when clearly shown. (N.W.P.S.)

The Lizzie Creek Cabin, which was built in 1968 by volunteers, sees greater stress upon it come winter. Your help in maintaining this public use cabin is essential if it is to continue serving everyone. Please clean up after yourselves, pack-out all garbage and food (the resident rat is well fed), hang up the foam pads, and close the shutters and doors securely when you leave. Also, the volunteer cut firewood supply is limited, so please use the stove sparingly.

Avalanche hazards of special note are the slopes immediately east of the cabin, Arrowhead Mountain's northwest-facing slopes, and the south-facing slopes between Cherry Pip Pass and Caltha Lake (the south slopes of Tundra Peak were appropriately nicknamed the "Terminator" by John Baldwin). Also beware of the large boulder fields found in this area, especially in the early months of winter.

On bad weather days (and, of course, for the deepest powder), good tree-skiing is found north of the cabin, while directly below Arrowhead Lake fantastic tree skiing is reported. White Lupine Ridge, which extends south from Anemone Peak, provides excellent skiing and can be reached by skiing directly up the forested slopes behind the cabin (watch for avalanche danger when exiting the trees at the top). Further along this ridge, the 2100 m (7000 ft) col between Anemone Peak and Tabletop Mountain leads to a large snowfield on the northwest side and more great slopes. The open country around Arrowhead Lake, Heart Lake, and Long Lake is worth exploring. The peaks and slopes east and southwest of Long Lake make for enjoyable touring, especially in times of high avalanche hazard. Those wanting a more challenging and lengthy ascent will consider Cloudraker to the southwest - a very long day-trip or comfortable two day return trip from the cabin.

Food for thought:

One loop trip that may be worth trying in times of relatively stable snow pack is via Lizzie Lake and Cherry Pip pass. Gain the pass from the Lizzie drainage. Descend from the pass to the valley to the north (your major concern here will be the volatile slopes of Tundra Peak above) and gain Bellevista Ridge. Proceed north to Meadow Dome and then descend to the logging road west of Meadow Dome. The road then switchbacks down to within 1 km of the start of the Lizzie Creek Road.

A longer and much more ambitious venture is found on the south divide of the Stein Watershed. This trip has only been done once in winter. In late March 1990, we were able to complete the entire trip from Lillooet Lake to the Fraser River via Log Creek in only eight days, with generous help from the weather gods. Count on at least seven days travel and allow for up to two weeks (if the weather closes in, your exit routes are limited and lengthy).

Starting at Lizzie Creek, move east to Caltha Lake and then southeast to Figure Eight Lake, south of Tundra Lake, where the divide portion of the trip begins. Some route-finding is required as you travel in a southeast direction to the glacier east of Mount Skook Jim, elevation 2580 m (8600 ft). Proceed east of Mt. Skook Jim along the glaciers which sit on the north side of the divide. Crevasse Crag and Mount Klackarpun are easily climbed along this section. The views are truly incredible from this section - perhaps the most spectacular of the entire trip.

The crux of the trip begins approximately 5.0 km east of Mount Klackarpun and extends to roughly 2.5 km west of the terminus of the Rutledge Glacier. Moderately steep snow

Deep Sleep

One of nature's least understood mysteries is a bear's ability to go into a dormant state for up to six months. Surviving off the accumulated fat layers, bears consume approximately 1 kj (5000 calories) per day during hibernation. How they can maintain this high metabolic rate for such a long time without eating or drinking is not entirely understood. Some insights have been gained through recent research, however. Apparently bears convert their urea - a by-product of the burning of food and normally unloaded as urine - into proteins. Thus, muscle mass is maintained and toxic buildups of urea are avoided. Similarly, females nurse their cubs during dormancy without drinking. If the mother bear is to produce milk, she requires water. The metabolizing of fat, which produces water, may be the source of fluids the sow needs.

Snowshoe hare
(Lepus americanus)
This primarily nocturnal bunny is common in forests, emerging at twilight to begin covering its 6 - 7 hectare range. The brown or greyish summer coat turns all white except for the ear tips come winter, making its camoflauge effective throughout the year. (N.B.)

slopes necessitate climbing and downclimbing several sections as you move along the ridge proper until above the three lakes in the basin above the north arm of Mehatl Creek. Once north of the eastern most of the aforementioned lakes, move on the south-facing slopes of the divide. A ramp south-southeast of the easternmost lake brings you over the divide and into the Rutledge Creek drainage.

At this point the route-finding becomes easier. Sidehill in an easterly direction to the Rutledge Glacier, which you then ascend to the south side of Kwoiek Peak in order to gain the Kwoiek and Chochiwa Glaciers. The easiest exit appears to be via the tongue of the Chochiwa Glacier that extends eastward into Log Creek. A logging road reaches to within about 3.5 km of the west end of the valley bottom. The Nahatlatch River Valley is eventually gained via this road.

Winter hiking

The Stein's lower canyon offers year-round hiking opportunities. Normally this dry area receives no more than 10 - 15 cm of snow, allowing for relatively easy travel. Beyond the cable crossing, however, the snowfalls are greater and skis or snowshoes are essential. Ensure you have lots of warm clothing - the sun does not warm the valley bottom for long in the winter. Wildlife viewing can be worthwhile at this time of year as mule deer, grouse, chickadees, nuthatches, and dippers frequent the lower canyon.

Winter camping in the lower Stein (D.T.)

PART VI:

THE POLITICS

OF PRESERVATION

TO PROTECT THE STEIN

Many different groups have worked for years to help protect the Stein from logging. Roy Mason, of the B.C. Mountaineering Club, made the first public effort when he submitted a private brief to the government in December 1973. Endorsed by the B.C. Wildlife Federation and reinforced by a similar request from the Federation of Mountain Clubs of B.C., this brief was the catalyst for a two-year moratorium on logging and mining in the Stein, which gave the government time to study the situation further.

Skeptical of the ensuing provincial government study, the F.M.C.B.C. conducted its own study, which was, in the words of the Parks Branch Director, "an outstanding....private proposal." Unfortunately, the newly- elected Socred government of 1976 ignored the recommendations of both the F.M.C.B.C.'s report and its own *Stein Basin Moratorium Study*'s recommendation that the Stein's timber be removed from the annual allowable cut. Adhering to its traditional "multiple-use" approach, the government announced in May 1976 that the Stein was to be logged.

> *"It is a long time since British Columbians hiked through timbered valleys or paddled by tree-lined shores. So long in fact that they accept tree stumps, logging slash, and drowned shorelines as standard. There are no lakes under 2500 feet in altitude within 100 miles of Vancouver that have not been logged to the shoreline, dammed or both. Not one. Not Pitt, nor Alouette, Chilliwack, Bunsen, Buttle, Dickson, Sproat, Stave, Weaver, Alta, Chehalis, Horne, Nahatlatch, Alice, Norton - none. There is only one major valley within 100 miles of Vancouver that has not been logged, flooded or both. Only one. It is the valley of the Stein River. It's just that simple. By the year 2000 - just 27 years from now - there will be three million people within a 3 hour drive of the Stein basin. How can we afford not to preserve this area.....?"*
>
> Roy Mason, December 4, 1973. From the first submission made to the provincial government on the future of the Stein River Valley by the Federation of Mountain Clubs of B.C.

In response to this decision and to the release of the government's inadequate Stein Basin Moratorium Study in October 1976, conservationists came together in March 1977 to form the Save the Stein Coalition. Representing more than 15 organizations and 45,000 individuals, the Coalition proved to be the stalwart of the fight for preservation for the next eight years. The Stein gained a tremendous boost in profile and accessibility with the Coalition's publication of *Exploring the Stein River Valley* (Roger Freeman and David Thompson), a thorough and well-researched guidebook. Newspapers and magazines began to focus on the Stein and public interest in this previously unknown wilderness increased.

At the same time, the Coalition pressed the Forest Service for the creation of the Stein River Public Liaison Committee. Unfortunately, as is the case with many advisory groups, both this committee and its successor, the Public Advisory Committee, were limited in their terms of reference in affecting decisions at the political level. Despite its broad powers, the Forest Service was bound by the political decision to log the Stein. Equally time-consuming and frustrating for the Coalition members was their successful fight to stop Ken Morris, a mining developer, from building a mine access road into the Stein.

In 1984 the Stein Advisory Committee released its Stein River Resource Folio. With the debate gaining momentum, the F.M.C.B.C. released *Wilderness or Logging: Case Studies of Two Conflicts in B.C.* (Trevor Jones). This study questioned not only the volumes of merchantable timber within the Stein, but also the profitability and subsidization of the proposed logging.

A significant development in the preservation campaign came in 1985. In February of that year, following the Forest Ministry's announcement that road-building would begin as soon as possible, local citizens and natives became part of a growing grass roots movement. A prominent feature of this new force was the first "Voices for the Wilderness" festival. Sponsored by the Lillooet Tribal Council and publicized by the Western Canada Wilderness Committee, the festival brought together 500 people at Brimful Lake for 3 days of entertainment and speeches.

Recognition of the native people's concerns was finally achieved when the government's 1986 Wilderness Advisory Committee recommended that "[a] road should not be constructed through the Stein River Canyon without a formal agreement between the Lytton Indian Band and the Provincial Government." The ground swell of public support convinced the government that the Stein was a major wilderness preservation and human rights issue worthy of further consideration.

> *"I feel pain and anger that the ancestors, the grandmothers and the grandfathers were so neglected when they offered up the best of their collective wisdom, their sacred rituals, and ceremonies and songs, for you to better understand the laws of the world you thought you had civilized. I feel pain and anger that in your rush towards development, the fabric of this globe has been rent, and what you call biosphere or ecosphere - but which my people more simply call Mother - has been so neglected and so hurt... I've heard grand talk of a new coalition of industry, scientists, governments and environmentalists from all over the world who will now finally work together to save our planet... Not once have I heard expressed the idea that indigenous people should be included in this grand coalition of humanity."*
>
> Chief Ruby Dunstan of the Lytton Band speaking at Globe '90 Conference, March 1990, Vancouver, B.C.

Meanwhile, Meares Island and South Moresby were firmly established on the national agenda, heightening awareness of wilderness preservation issues and indigenous people's concerns. The work of the Lytton and Mt. Currie Bands under the courageous leadership of Lytton and Mt. Currie Chiefs Dunstan and Andrew intensified in 1988. A series of meetings between the provincial government and the Lytton band, an unprecedented visit by the Chiefs to New Zealand in November to address Fletcher Challenge shareholders, and the tremendous success of the bands' festivals brought national coverage to what had been until then a provincial issue. Equally effective in helping create greater awareness were the efforts of environmental organizations, in particular Western Canada Wilderness Committee's public education and trail-building programs, and the publication of *Stein: The Way of the River* (Michael M'Gonigle and Wendy Wickwire, 1988).

> *"Our position, which will never waver, is to maintain the forests of the Stein Valley in their natural state forever; to share our valley with other life forms equally; but also to share the valley with those people who can bring to the Stein a respect for the natural life there similar to that taught us by our ancestors."*
>
> Excerpt from Lytton & Mt. Currie Indian Bands' "Stein Declaration", October, 1987.

The increase in awareness and support for preservation of the Stein, and the reluctance of the government to negotiate with the Lytton Band prompted Fletcher Challenge, the company wanting to log the Stein, to declare a one year moratorium on any further logging preparation in April 1989. At this point, the future of the Stein looked better. The company's "backdoor option" - building an access road through the North Stein - remains a threat, however. In the spring of 1989 the Lytton and Mt. Currie Bands unveiled plans for a Stein Tribal Heritage Park with a cultural interpretation centre or museum sited at the mouth of the Stein.

Comparison of 1986 Employment per Volume Harvested: B.C., Northwest U.S., and Sweden (jobs per 1000 cubic metres).

B.C	1.06	Idaho	2.01	Montana	1.44
Oregon	1.92	Washington	1.92	Alaska	1.05
Sweden	2.20				

Sources: Council of Forest Industries, B.C Forest Industry Fact Book; Statistics Canada, Selected Forestry Statistics 1987; USDA Forest Service 1987; and Swedish Forest Industry Public Communications 1988.

The shocking truth regarding B.C.'s mismanaged forests and diminishing wilderness areas has become a major public concern. While the wilderness preservation movement is gaining momentum on a global scale, a sense of urgency prevails regarding protection of the Stein Valley and other remaining wilderness areas. Protection of complete ecosystems is of utmost importance if we are to preserve a liveable planet. In B.C. we must do our part in the global campaign to protect wilderness. Currently, only 2% of B.C.'s forests are protected and less than 6% of the total land base has been designated as park, wilderness area, or ecological reserve. Furthermore, the annual allowable cut has grown from 6.7 million cubic metres in 1912 to an historic high of 90.5 million cubic metres in 1987 with reforestation lagging far behind. The pressure on B.C.'s forests has never been greater.

In response to this crisis and the need to move quickly, a number of environmental organizations have begun working on comprehensive wilderness protection programs. Western Canada Wilderness Committee's WILD project is preparing an inventory of the Earth's endangered wilderness areas. Nationally, the World Wildlife Fund's Endangered Spaces Campaign is working to ensure that 12% of Canada's land base and marine areas is protected by the year 2000. In 1988 the Valhalla Society put forward a proposal to protect a total of 13.1% of B.C.'s land base.

This proposal, which garnered considerable attention from government, industry, and the public, was studied by the Natural Resources Management Program at Simon Fraser University. *Wilderness and Forestry: Assessing the Cost of Comprehensive Wilderness Protection in B.C.* confirmed what many environmentalists have been claiming: Reduction of both the net land area available for timber harvesting and the annual allowable cut would be insignificant (4.7% and 3.5% respectively). Furthermore, these "losses" could be more than offset by other policies including improved silviculture, greater timber utilization, and value-added manufacturing. In other words, we can have more protected wilderness and still have logging and other industrial activities.

In light of the increasing pressures on our land base, governments must take quick action to protect our remaining wilderness areas. The 1990s is the last decade in which we will have this opportunity. As has been the case in past conservation campaigns, concerned citizens, not politicians, will be the leaders. Supporting environmental and native organizations working for wilderness preservation and aboriginal concerns, and writing letters to politicians are two of the easier and more effective ways concerned individuals can help. The Minister of Forests and the Premier can be contacted at: Parliament Buildings, Victoria, B.C. V8V 1X4. In B.C., the Stikine, Khutzeymateen, Carmanah, Clayoquot Sound, Chilcotin, Tatshenshini, Kitlope, and Stein are but a few of the high profile places needing protection. Your support has never been more in demand than now.

Space limitations do not allow for a complete listing of wilderness preservation and native organizations. For more information on these issues and concerned organizations contact:

B.C. Environmental Network, 2150 Maple Street, Vancouver, B.C. V6J 3T3 (604) 733-2400

Union of B.C. Indian Chiefs, 200 - 73 Water Street, Vancouver, B.C. V6B 1A1 (604) 684-0231

Valhalla Society, Box 224 New Denver, B.C. V0G 1S0 (604) 358-2449

Western Canada Wilderness Committee, 20 Water Street, Vancouver, B.C. V6B 1A4 (604) 683-8220

EPILOGUE

Since the Stein became a political issue, now almost 20 years ago, there have always been a few people who have spent time in the valley, heard its voice of nature and of reason, and acted. From the time 17 years ago when David Thompson and Roger Freeman bushwhacked mile after weary mile through an unknown wilderness while writing the first guidebook, *Exploring the Stein River Valley* (now out of print) to Gordon's solo ventures writing this new guidebook, more and more people have come to discover the magic of the river, and to act on its behalf.

There is Ken Lay of the Western Canada Wilderness Committee who spent seven weeks, often alone, building a trail through the Stein's main valley. Or Leo deGroot, a pioneer of the early Rediscovery program, skiing in the dead of winter along high alpine ridges, then down the long side-valleys. And Morgan Wells and Rod Dunstan of the Mt. Currie and Lytton Bands respectively, Rediscovery leaders who have grown up in the area, able to explore the one magnificent bit of whole wilderness still left in their peoples' ancestral home.

And there is now a whole new generation growing up with the Stein. What is this generation experiencing? Truth, nothing short of the truth.

Imagine the scene. You are alone, the others are unpacking. Tired from climbing or walking, you are sitting by the swift, quiet currents of that clear mountain river as it meanders beneath the towering cottonwoods swaying in the breeze. In such all too rare moments in life today, you can see, hear, smell, and feel nature at its purest and most alive.

Or you are in the alpine, sitting on a clump of boulders near the top of the ridge. There, below you, in the open meadow of a rich soggy sidecreek, a grizzly snorts and paws the bushes, eating berries, almost oblivious to its surroundings.

To witness, to be part of, life in such vibrancy, to experience that moment is to begin, ever so slowly, to understand the native voice. Mind, body, and nature as one. Spirit as connectedness outward. At such times, the river really does speak. And even now at the cold plastic keyboard of the computer, the memory refreshes.

We are entering a time of great social upheaval and change. We cannot separate the Stein from Carmanah, from the Amazon rainforest, or even the diminishing ozone layer. We are a planetary culture devouring our planetary home. To change direction, we must begin again to know where we live, to learn to respect and love our own local places. Reforming the planet must truly begin at home.

The experience of a sacred moment in the Stein is, we said, building a whole new generation. Especially for the people of the area - Mt. Currie, Lillooet, Lytton, - this is a generation with growing local knowledge. Their experiences in the Stein provide the attitudes and the skill that might allow us all to learn to work with our heritage - not destroy it for a quick buck.

Those who read this book, and spend time in the Stein, will join a growing movement of change. There are still incredible opportunities in the Stein, and in the wider world as well. But we do not have much time.

In Lytton, and everywhere else for that matter, we need a new, sustainable, economic base. The Stein can, in part, provide that. Already hiking companies and kayakers are working or assessing the valley's business potential. Meanwhile, the bands are looking at a very imaginative form of tourist facility using traditional architecture. And the Rediscovery program is providing new young leaders, native and non-native, who can act as guides, and especially as resource managers.

That the Stein must be preserved is obvious, even for economic reasons. Politically, the demand for its protection is evident, for example, in the swelling support for the annual Stein festivals (ably organized by John McCandless year after year). The Chiefs, Kathy Wallace of Mt. Currie, and Byron Spinks of Lytton, have long known that it must be preserved, and have told us so.

But with potential comes the concern that, whatever we do in the Stein, we must be guided by respect. Again, spending time in the valley will be the best assurance of our developing that respect.

But the Stein is also the community which surrounds and protects it. When we wrote our own book about the Stein, we did so as much out of a love for that community, as for the valley. Many readers will know, for example, Louis Phillips, Hilda Austin, Jimmy Scotchman, and Charlie Mack from past Stein festivals. These great people are part of a community whose history and very possibility for a future lives with that valley. Every home on the west side of the Fraser has its connection with the Stein. In most of the Indian houses in the area, the Wilderness Committee's Stein poster, Joy to the World, hangs with pride on the living room wall.

Whatever we do, we must respect, and empower, the community as well. The whole community, native and non-native alike. Here again, only an economy that both works with nature and involves diverse segments of the population can bring our communities together. Sustainability is again the key. Stable community and culture cannot exist without it.

To preserve the Stein our dwindling world demands big social change. Such places must be saved for many reasons. One is so that people can go there, learn, and be refreshed. And then come back and make a different world.

Take this book and learn to love the Stein, and in the process help make the ecological transition on which everything else depends.

Michael M'Gonigle and Wendy Wickwire

" I think that we have to struggle to find a way to celebrate, both here in B.C. and in the Amazon, and all the ecosystems of the world, the fact that we are now a single planet. That we are no longer a place where we can look to the great frontiers. We must really remember that image that Story Musgrave gave from space, that image of the floating planet. An image that will transform the philosophical foundations of our lives much more than even the Copernican revolution did 500 years ago, which suggested that the planet was no longer the centre of the solar system. What we see from space then is this single interactive sphere of life. We see a planet that some of us like to call Gaia. We see the only house we have and it seems to me that the only thing worth doing in these small, short, rather insignificant lives we have, is to struggle to protect that world from the marauders of our own species."

Ethnobotanist Wade Davis speaking at a Vancouver Tropical Rainforest Action Society presentation, September 21, 1989.

PART VII:

REFERENCES

Selected Bibliography

General

- Freeman, Roger, and Thompson, David. *Exploring the Stein River Valley*, Douglas & McIntyre, 1979.
- McGonigle, Michael, and Wickwire, Wendy. *Stein: The Way of the River*, Talon Books, 1988.
- Natural Resources Management Program, Simon Fraser University. *Wilderness and Forestry: Assessing the Cost of Comprehensive Wilderness Protection in B.C.*, 1990.
- Department of Recreation and Conservation, B.C. Parks Branch. *The Stein Basin Moratorium Study*, 1976.
- Turner, Nancy, et al.. *Thompson Ethnobotany*. Royal B.C. Museum, 1990.

Backcountry Travel, Ethics, and Safety

- Hampton, Bruce, and Cole, David. *Soft Paths*, Stackpole Books, 1988.
- Herrero, Stephen. *Bear Attacks: Their Causes and Avoidance*, Nick Lyon Books, 1985.
- Manning, Harvey. *Backpacking: One Step at a Time*, Vintage Books, 1980.
- Peters, Ed. *Mountaineering: The Freedom of the Hills,* The Mountaineers, 1982.

Natural History

- Ade, R. *The Trout and Salmon Handbook*. Facts on File, Inc., 1989.
- Cowan, Ian McTaggart, and Guiguet, Charles J. *The Mammals of B.C.*, B.C. Provincial Museum, 1978.
- Duddington, C.L. *Beginner's Guide to The Fungi*. Pelham Books, 1972.
- Gadd, Ben. *Handbook of the Canadian Rockies*, Corax Press, 1986.
- Goward, Trevor, and Hickson, Cathie. *Nature Wells Gray*, Friends of Wells Gray Park, 1989.
- Hale, M.E. *How to Know the Lichens*. 2nd ed. Wm.C. Brown Co., 1979.
- Horst, Vicki. "The Pika," *Canadian Geographic*, Aug/Sept., 1986
- Klasson, Michael. "The Last Stand of the Cottonwoods," Canadian Nature Federation, Winter, 1990.
- Lynch, Wayne. "The Elusive Cougar," *Canadian Geographic*, Aug/Sept., 1989.
- Lyons, C.P. *Trees, Shrubs, and Flowers to Know in B.C.*, J.M. Dent and Sons, 1976.
- Maser, Chris. *Forest Primeval*. Sierra Club Books, 1989.
- Peterson, Roger T. *A Field Guide to Western Birds*. Houghton Mifflin Co., 1961.
- Scott, W.B. and Crossman, E.J. *Freshwater Fishes of Canada*, bulletin 184. Fisheries Research Board of Canada, 1973.
- Vitt, D.H., Marsh, J.E. and Bovey, R.B. *Mosses, Lichens & Ferns of Northwest America*. Lone Pine Publishing, 1988.
- Whitaker, John O. Jr. *The Audubon Society Field Guide to North American Mammals*, Alfred A. Knopf, Inc., 1980.
- Willoughby, L. *Freshwater Biology*. Hutchinson of London, 1976.
- Yalden, D.W. and P.A. Morris. *The Lives of Bats*, David Charles Ltd., 1975.

Martin Roland

Waiting for the Second Flooding

The author developed his passion for the outdoors exploring the dry Interior near his home town of Kamloops. A graduate of the University of British Columbia with a B.A. in political science, Gordon is now combining his love of writing and the outdoors in working towards protecting endangered wilderness areas. His future plans include writing more books. He currently resides in Vancouver.

Additional copies of the fold-out map can be ordered for $5.00 each. Please send orders to:

Stein Wilderness Alliance
2150 Maple St.
Vancouver, B.C. V6J 3T3